Grit, Grind, & Grace

ACTIVATE IT!

By

TOWANDA R. LIVINGSTON

"Towandaism"

Published by Write the Book Now, an imprint of Perfect Time SHP LLC.

DEDICATION

"To God be the GLORY!"

I dedicate this priceless piece of me to my Mother, Denise ("Niecy") McNeil, my Husband (my ROCK), Bryan and my Daughter, Bryce. Also, this book is dedicated to my awesome niece, Lyric; my sensational Sister, Tanesha and my God-given Father, Gerald (Roy). My Mother-In-Love, Eileen Gibbons, words cannot express how grateful I am for her love; and for supporting and loving me through my messes.

Special Thank You to *my Sisters in Success*, Wendy Archer and Jennifer Gray! Thank you for pushing me into my purpose! It is a powerful evolution when the teacher becomes the student of her students; you have inspired me more than you will ever know.

Thank you to my anointed intercessory, Dina Nance Bell. Your unwavering spiritual guidance helps raise the broken girl in me to a worthy woman.

Preface

As I am writing this book I am going through the darkest days of my life, yet I have faith. I find myself in a tsunami of never-ending storms that are meant to destroy me at my core and erase me and all I have accomplished thus far (*this is not the finish line it is the starting line for living my BEST life*); yet and still I have hope. I am being bombarded with self-destructive and self-sabotaging thoughts and sometimes actions; yet and still I act with love. Every second is a battle, not just to breathe but to thrive; and yet and still I spread grace in abundance. I must share what I am going through at this very moment, so that you can know that whatever you are going through you are not alone and you WILL make it, all you have to do is **ACT**, **MOVE** and **PUSH** forward. I subscribe to the belief that, "either by inspiration or desperation, you will be **PUSHED** into your **PURPOSE**!" Therefore, at this very moment you are being shaped, molded, and transformed into your greatest self. Your breakthrough moment has arrived! You are anointed for this time, reason and season; now it is time to claim your rightful appointment; and all you need to pack for this journey is grace, grit and your inherent ability to grind.

> *"To be a fisher of women and men through servitude so that they can realize and appreciate their God–given greatness by walking in their purpose, passion and possibilities for their lives."*
> – Towanda R. Livingston's Personal Mission Statement

Unfortunately, the only way to sustainable success and prosperity is through pain. It is through pain folks find their purpose. "Everyone wants to be a diamond, but no one wants to get cut…in order for diamonds to shine brilliantly they must be cut and the process is not easy." Once you have defined and surrendered to your purpose, nothing can and will stop you from achieving your PURPOSE! Now, it has to be your purpose and not someone else's or society's purpose for you. Building your emotional muscle, rallying all of the Davids you will need to slay all of the Goliaths you will encounter on the road to your legacy is paramount. I need you to dig deep within yourself and activate the champion, game-changer, and warrior that is already in you. Enough is enough, it is time for you to become a champion among men and a warrior among women. We are not taking any P.O.Ws (Prisoners of War), we are unleashing all of our talents and greatness on this world, because we have nothing to lose and everything to gain. When we see successful folks, we think they are born that way or better yet an overnight success, now that is funny; however, success is like an iceberg, the world sees the peak of the iceberg, however they do not see what is under the waterline or all that person went through to achieve success in their life. We don't see the rising tide or the heat that threatens this success daily and has tried to consume the iceberg – all that has to continuously be done to achieve sustainable success. Just because achieving success is hard work we must not be deterred.

Here is the deal, someone in the world needs for you to fulfill your purpose so that they can realize theirs. Your greatest opportunities are ahead of you, it doesn't matter how many poor (or FUBAR -*fucked up beyond all recognition.*) choices you have made in the past, if the sun rises on you, you are one of the fortunate people who have another chance to get it right and get on course to living your **BEST** life. Every saint has a past and every sinner has a future. I don't believe in watering dead plants, so living and re-living the past is a waste of valuable time; shrinking yourself so you melt away into the background is not in your DNA; and failing is not an option.

Your endless possibilities start in your mind, your mind is the most fertile place in the universe, it is trillion times more fertile than earth's healthiest soil. Therefore, whatever you plant in your mind will grow exponentially, so if you plant weeds of self-doubt, self-hate, I can'ts – this will grow and will manifest in your life; **HOWEVER**, if you plant positive thoughts for example, I got this, I am a champion, I am independently wealthy and financial secure, I am intelligent, I am brilliant etc…this will not only grow but produce endless fruit. Speaking of "I am" statements, surround yourself with them, post them all around your home, office, social platform and more importantly plant them in you. Your "I am" statements will put a demand on heaven and the universe to unleash your blessings, successes and prosperity.

The purpose of this book is to activate you daily, to transform you into a success savage, a wealth warrior, and a prosperity prophet. It does not matter your position in life, or what you are going through or preparing for, with faith, hope, purpose and taking action you can claim victory **NOW!** All you have to do is **ACTIVATE**!

I created "Towandaisms" to plant seeds of aspiration, inspiration and motivation into you, our world, and the universe - to manifest into a tsunami of never-ending abundance. I want all the "greats" for you: love, joy, success, prosperity, happiness, peace… In order to claim all of that is *impossible*, I need you to get your mind right to get your grind right; I need you to be hungry for the hustle; I need you to **ACTIVATE**!

No matter what you going through at this very moment, health issues, financial issues, family-related issues, workplace issues, internal battles, spiritual battles or **WHATEVER** the battle; this is not the end, this is not the finish line, your story does not end here, so **GET** UP off the mat, and **GET** off your ass and **ACTIVATE** your dreams! I know it may feel like you are drowning, or stagnant, or becoming a part of the living-dying (*those folks that are in a permanent nod state and have become drones and sheep*); I am asking you to go deep within yourself, and yes this is both hard work and heart work, and make **FAITH** an action word in your life and **MOVE!** It does not matter what life is throwing at you, does not matter the size of the storm, does not matter the trials of tribulations…all you have to do is MOVE with expectations and faith. Take baby steps or quantum leaps, just **MOVE**. See, it is hard to hit a moving target, don't become an easy target and **MOVE** now! If you are struggling, start small and **GET UP** and wash your face, brush your teeth and more importantly wash your ass. These acts of self-care are the foundation of taking care of everything else you will encounter daily; and demonstrating to God and the Universe you are preparing for success and you are ready for your tsunami of successes. This is your time, so ***ACTIVATE!*** ***"Keep Shining and Showing Up Great!"***

Foreword Flow

God's Word Is Life! The Lord says in John 1:1-4, "In the Beginning was the Word, and the Word was with God, and the Word was God. He was with God in the beginning. Through him all things were made; without him nothing was made that has been made. In him was life, and that life was the light of all mankind." This powerful passage depicts that even before the earth was formed, the Word was already in existence with the eternal one, God. It also gives us a clear picture that everyone that was made, was made through him. It also states that in him was life. As a result, I believe that anytime I read, mediate, study, share, believe, speak and obey his Word, I shall have life!

Over nineteen years ago, God began to speak into my spirit about a business that would be focused on training individuals in various topics. As the next few years moved forward, he began to bring clarity to the vision and share with me that while I would start a new business, I would also incorporate ministry into everything I would do for this business. Please know that none of this made sense to me because I was new in Christ and I was very comfortable in my full time Project Management and Training Consulting role at a pretty large Consulting Company and had no desire to depart from it. But remember, God's Word is Life. As I began to seek him for clarity and wisdom on my next career move, he began to lead me in a different path. And before I knew it, he sent mentors, coaches and friends to help me dissect the Word and the Instruction. In June 2002, Training by Design, Inc. was birthed.

During the first three years of business, there were many, many things the Lord spoke into my spirit as I moved around in a daze trying to figure out if I had lost my mind in this transition. But as I began to build a grind, I started asking many, many questions from anybody I inquired about how to find a great mentor or coach and who should I connect with - and one comment and name that continued to come up in many conversations was, "Have you had a chance to meet Towanda Livingston." At that time, Towanda was described as pretty much the same way she is described now:

- ❖ A Powerhouse;
- ❖ A Phenomenal and Compassionate leader;
- ❖ A Woman Committed to Excellence;
- ❖ A Leader in the Supplier & Diversity space;
- ❖ A Person Committed to Growing Small Businesses & Building Partnerships;

❖ A Woman Committed to Changing the World – through One Small Business at A Time!

After a few of these discussions, I made it my business to meet her. I reached out to the Agency she was supporting to find out when she was scheduled to attend the next Conference, Outreach Session or Workshop and as a result, I attended them as well. Because there was always a line at her table, or a crowd gathered around her, I waited, waited and waited until either the end of that event or the next event. But while waiting, I always left knowing that she was a Woman of Excellence who was compassionate and she would have a Word for me that would help grow my company! And I was correct.

Once I had the first opportunity to actually meet Towanda at a Conference, I was overwhelmed. She shared nuggets and wisdom on growing my business but also gave me assignments, attention and an ear to share my struggles. I truly believe that this powerful book: "Grit, Grind and Grace" was born on that day at least 13 – 14 years ago along with her nuggets of wisdom known as "Towandaisms". As time went on, we spoke, met, brainstormed, strategized and connected, but each session became a time of Mentoring, Coaching and Connecting. She then began to empower, engage and encourage me as she reminded me that I am truly walking in my purpose and nothing can stop me from moving forward. At one of our business meetings, I recognized that we needed to pray because her Words were going after my fears and inadequacies and I would not leave this meeting the same. As I began to depart from her office, I remember thinking, I can't wait to read her first book because I know hundreds of lives will be changed! And quickly after that meeting, I noticed that Towanda began to share her powerful words of wisdom and encouragement to the world on Social Media. I began to seek them out daily, share them, meditate on them, print them, speak them and believe the content that they were displaying.

Executives, Leaders, Small Business Owners and the World need "Grit, Grind and Grace!" I believe the Lord has placed a mandate on Towanda's life for sharing wisdom, instruction and love to empower, equip and educate you as you push through the fire, the struggles and the setbacks. Whether you are starting a powerful and international small business, enhancing your current consulting assignment, working full time in your government office, transitioning into retirement, at home taking care of your most precious assets in your children or just trying to enjoy your life, allow "Grit, Grind and Grace" to be your Daily Devotion and Guide to handling adversity while walking in your purpose in this season!

Dina Bell Nance, Chief Learning Officer
Training by Design, Inc. – "Where God Is The CEO!"
10405 Blackstone Avenue, Cheltenham, MD 20623
Email: Nancetd@aol.com
Web: www.TrainingbyDesignInc.com
Contact: 301-640-1203

Sit at the TABLE!

Guidance

You must meditate and journal in order to get the most out of this book. As you read each Towandaism, at a minimum one daily, I strongly encourage you to meditate and journal what you are feeling, thinking and more importantly how you will ACTIVATE, MOVE and pursue your greatness and purpose. My preference is to meditate and journal in the morning to command my day; however, you have to do what works for you. Since all days are not created equal, sometimes I find myself meditating or journaling throughout the day to bring balance and order to my life so I am not thrown off course (goal-focused and forward-focused only) and consumed by mass distractions. I have divided this book into themes which will make it easier for you to locate the activation words you need to press on, press into your purpose, lean into the journey and push through the pain or struggle. This journey is all about YOU, designed for YOU and will work through YOU, just surrender--you have nothing to lose and everything to gain in love.

Journaling is very important to your growth development, and in some cases sanity. Be creative about your journaling. You can draw, paste collages, write, blog, video, or record; or a mixture of all of these. To support you with journaling, each Towandaism is accompanied by the **ACTIVATION** lure to instigate your greatness daily:

i.   **Envision IT** – paint the picture in your mind, visualize it, and see yourself crushing it.

ii. **Manifest IT** – make real by showing up GREAT.

iii. **ACTIVATE IT** – Do, ACT, Do, ACT! Keep going no matter what!

iv. What's going to be your **"go-to" word** today? - The word that is going to keep you focus on crushing your activation goal(s) for the day, the next second, minute or hour. This word (or mantra) is going to refocus you when you are bombarded with mass distractions throughout the day.

"This is a participatory healing, learning and growing process. Get off your ass NOW, get out of your emotions, get out of your past...Let's get to work and ride this muthafucka until the wheels fall off!" – Towandaism

What are Towandaisms?

Well, Towandaisms are derived from how I walk through life with faith and favor; I created my "isms'' to combat the negative "isms" that continue to hold folks back from achieving their greatness. I authored Towandaisms to activate the beast mode in YOU and to push YOU into pursuing, relentlessly, all that God has promised YOU. – Towandaism

GRIT - Purposefulness

Grit-The Journey begins

"There are four words you will never hear God say, "You are a mistake." YOU are purposefully designed for a time such as this." – Towandaism

Envision IT!

Manifest IT!

ACTIVATE IT!

What's going to be your "go-to" word today?

"What you are going **THROUGH** is to help you to increase and improve your capacity for where you are going, not to keep you where you're **AT!!!**" – Towandaism

Envision IT!

Manifest IT!

ACTIVATE IT!

What's going to be your "go-to" word today?

"Today, I am 'faithing' it until I make it!" – Towandaism

Envision IT!

Manifest IT!

ACTIVATE IT!

What's going to be your "go-to" word today?

"What is God's heartbeat for you? *Lean into it.*" – Towandaism

Envision IT!

Manifest IT!

ACTIVATE IT!

What's going to be your "go-to" word today?

"The path I chose was not perfect, it was filled with painful dizzying twists and turns, but still I persist."
– Towandaism

Envision IT!

Manifest IT!

ACTIVATE IT!

What's going to be your "go-to" word today?

"Celebrate your WINS! When we under-praise ourselves, we fall short of the glory of God. So, celebrate, shout, cheer and applaud you and your journey!" – Towandaism

Envision IT!

Manifest IT!

ACTIVATE IT!

What's going to be your "go-to" word today?

"Effort does not equate to impact." – Towandaism

Envision IT!

Manifest IT!

ACTIVATE IT!

What's going to be your "go-to" word today?

"I know times are tough right now, so, it's okay to VENT, let it all out; and then LET IT GO! See, it is actually healthy to vent in a 'safe harbor'; what is not healthy, is you choosing to stay in that cathartic state—it's not okay for you to wallow in your frustrated state and recruit others, unknowingly, to join you. Acknowledge it! Vent it! & Surrender it! Claim your joy!" – Towandaism

Envision IT!

Manifest IT!

ACTIVATE IT!

What's going to be your "go-to" word today?

"Today, I strongly encourage you to STOP and let God step in the situation. Watch God work!"

– Towandaism

Envision IT!

Manifest IT!

ACTIVATE IT!

What's going to be your "go-to" word today?

"Identity and integrity go hand-in-hand; once you know who you are you are then able to live it out unapologetically. You move differently when you are confident about your identity and the world moves differently around you when you live out loud." – Towandaism

Envision IT!

Manifest IT!

ACTIVATE IT!

What's going to be your "go-to" word today?

"My soul aches for it, I will do what it takes for it, I will never forsake it, I need to embrace it, I need to have faith in it, I will ride and live for it, you can't have it or use it, I have been appointed to it and anointed by it, damn, I can taste it! Purpose, purpose, purpose; yeah, that's IT!" – Towandaism

Envision IT!

Manifest IT!

ACTIVATE IT!

What's going to be your "go-to" word today?

"Other's faith in you will only take you but so far; however, when you have unwavering faith in yourself, you become unbounded, your possibilities become immeasurable and you take the limits off of God!"

– Towandaism

Envision IT!

Manifest IT!

ACTIVATE IT!

What's going to be your "go-to" word today?

"My Friend, Dream God-Sized Dreams and establish God-Sized Goals; and, walk with expectation. Then...Watch how God moves Destiny Builders, Purpose Promoters and Acceleration Advocates in your path. Your Time is NOW!" – Towandaism

Envision IT!

Manifest IT!

ACTIVATE IT!

What's going to be your "go-to" word today?

"The grass looks greener on the other side, however wherever the grass is greener the water bill is higher, the maintenance commitment is priority; SO, if you want to be successful you have to be prepared to pay the cost and commit without ceasing!"
– Towandaism

Envision IT!

Manifest IT!

ACTIVATE IT!

What's going to be your "go-to" word today?

"What if, God will close a door so that you cannot return to where you came from, and you have to deal with what is in front of you?" – Towandaism

Envision IT!

Manifest IT!

ACTIVATE IT!

What's going to be your "go-to" word today?

"Stop being a wound collector! Unload all those past wounds you have been lugging around; go ahead and lighten your load, forgive yourself, forgive others, release the guilt, release the jealousy, release the shame, so that, you can make space for God to work, make room for prosperity, success, and most importantly love." – Towandaism

Envision IT!

Manifest IT!

ACTIVATE IT!

What's going to be your "go-to" word today?

"Think about this--you have never lived this day before and you will never live it again. So, make this moment, this time, and this gift count! You have been blessed with another day to get it right; chase your dreams to love, to serve and to become— Use it or lose it my friend!" – Towandaism

Envision IT!

Manifest IT!

ACTIVATE IT!

What's going to be your "go-to" word today?

"My struggle is **REAL,** but so is my **GOD!** With unbroken progress, God has it covered and conquered!"

– Towandaism

Envision IT!

Manifest IT!

ACTIVATE IT!

What's going to be your "go-to" word today?

"Not everyone is going to 'catch the vision,' so surround yourself with folks who will support you—they may not see what your vision as clearly as you do, but they believe that you see it and will achieve it."

– Towandaism

Envision IT!

Manifest IT!

ACTIVATE IT!

What's going to be your "go-to" word today?

"I often wonder what our world would be like or how our lives would be different if Adam & Eve ate from the Tree of Life instead of the Tree of Knowledge in Eden." – Towandaism

Envision IT!

Manifest IT!

ACTIVATE IT!

What's going to be your "go-to" word today?

"My Mommy tried, hard, to instill in me that if you keep giving a man your money or taking care of a man; he will fall in love with your hand and not your heart. You can't buy life-giving, life-sustaining and life-affirming LOVE! Buying his love is not going to help you love yourself more." *With age comes wisdom.*

– Towandaism

Envision IT!

Manifest IT!

ACTIVATE IT!

What's going to be your "go-to" word today?

"Farmers who wait for perfect weather never plant. Similarly, if you are waiting for the right time to start your business, or to write that book, or to start your family, or to finish your education or pursue your wildest dreams—you will never do it! Do it now, start now! Arrest all thoughts of fear and procrastination and replace them with faith and winning!" – Towandaism

Envision IT!

Manifest IT!

ACTIVATE IT!

What's going to be your "go-to" word today?

"I am both grateful and broken and this gives me my flavor and the courage to press on, preserve and pursue by blessings relentlessly." – Towandaism

Envision IT!

Manifest IT!

ACTIVATE IT!

What's going to be your "go-to" word today?

"Sometimes a change in perspective requires a flip of your hair, instead of flipping the bird!" – Towandaism

Envision IT!

Manifest IT!

ACTIVATE IT!

What's going to be your "go-to" word today?

"It took uncommon women with uncommon courage to transform our world, laws, business, economies and cultures. So, playing it safe, hiding your talents, and staying down when life tries to beat down are not options! That common dress and those common shoes are no longer your size; and they are not the right fit for your uncommon journey!" – Towandaism

Envision IT!

Manifest IT!

ACTIVATE IT!

What's going to be your "go-to" word today?

"Victory without receipts, rewards or results is hollow. Overcoming, winning, and succeeding comes with tangible and intangible results and has both intrinsic and extrinsic value." – Towandaism

Envision IT!

Manifest IT!

ACTIVATE IT!

What's going to be your "go-to" word today?

"May prosperity chase you down and poverty never catch you, in the name and blood of Jesus!"
– Towandaism

Envision IT!

Manifest IT!

ACTIVATE IT!

What's going to be your "go-to" word today?

"Some Churches are great performers, that can put on a great Cirque du Soleil or Broadway show as if God's radical word has been provided to entertain you! The problem with this approach is that in order to keep your congregation entertained the show has to get better and better every week--Church or Fellowship in God's radical word is about receiving constant strength, sustenance and building emotional and spiritual muscles to defeat the persistent and daily attacks of the enemy. So, if you want to be entertained buy a ticket to a show; however, if you want to be renewed, transformed, redeemed, and blessed beyond measure you must embrace God's Radical Word!" – Towandaism

Envision IT!

Manifest IT!

ACTIVATE IT!

What's going to be your "go-to" word today?

"We have been conned into trading in our future greatness for complacency, conformity, consensus, contempt and comfort. Break these yokes and put your successes on flow!" – Towandaism

Envision IT!

Manifest IT!

ACTIVATE IT!

What's going to be your "go-to" word today?

"You can have all the knowledge in the world, have all the talent in the world and have all the resources to be successful on tap and fail miserably, derail yourself because you lack common sense." – Towandaism

Envision IT!

Manifest IT!

ACTIVATE IT!

What's going to be your "go-to" word today?

"Excellence, Success and Favor cost something; you will have to sow, invest or sacrifice something to live on purpose and achieve greatness." – Towandaism

Envision IT!

Manifest IT!

ACTIVATE IT!

What's going to be your "go-to" word today?

"Being broke is a trip I don't want to take and destination I don't want to visit; however, if I must, may the trip be short and painful with a purpose; and the destination so disgusting and uncomfortable that it PUSHES me into my GREATNESS!" – Towandaism

Envision IT!

Manifest IT!

ACTIVATE IT!

What's going to be your "go-to" word today?

"In order to be successful at anything, you must have and demonstrate courage. You must run towards your fears and obstacles: You must chase the lions; you must swim towards the sharks; and you must whip the wolves. You must be hungrier and more determined than the lion, shark and wolf in your pursuits."
– Towandaism

Envision IT!

Manifest IT!

ACTIVATE IT!

What's going to be your "go-to" word today?

"The entrepreneur spirit is strong in her/him!" – Towandaism

Envision IT!

Manifest IT!

ACTIVATE IT!

What's going to be your "go-to" word today?

"We have allowed the morally corrupt to morally bankrupt us, by allowing them to influence us with their watered-down interpretation of God's radical word and Jesus's radical message. We have allowed "shock jock" behaviors and sensationalism to make us passive participants in the spiritual decay of our values, families and communities. God's radical word does not have to conform to us and what we want; we have to conform, lean in and actively embrace Jesus's radical message and behaviors and disrupt the status quo!" – Towandaism

Envision IT!

Manifest IT!

ACTIVATE IT!

What's going to be your "go-to" word today?

"Thank you, God, for making what seems impossible to others, Possible for me and thank you God for making what seems supernatural to others, natural for me." – Towandaism

Envision IT!

Manifest IT!

ACTIVATE IT!

What's going to be your "go-to" word today?

"Pssst...you are dangerously and divinely worthy." – Towandaism

Envision IT!

Manifest IT!

ACTIVATE IT!

What's going to be your "go-to" word today?

"Purposeful Intentions are powerful; fill up your soul with your passion and then refill it." – Towandaism

Envision IT!

Manifest IT!

ACTIVATE IT!

What's going to be your "go-to" word today?

I read a Tweet: *"I just wanna be successful and stay out the way... I work hard as fuck!"*

My Reply: **"Your success puts you in the way; your hard work shows and makes it hard for others to ignore your greatness. One of the costs of success is interrupting the thoughts of others whose egos made them think they were successful and then you showed up. Keep Shining and Showing Up Great!" – Towandaism**

Envision IT!

Manifest IT!

ACTIVATE IT!

What's going to be your "go-to" word today?

"You're right, I'm not good enough, **I AM GREAT ENOUGH** and Unstoppable, I'll be at the **TOP** waiting for you!" – Towandaism

Envision IT!

Manifest IT!

ACTIVATE IT!

What's going to be your "go-to" word today?

"Get your mind right to get your grind right." – Towandaism

Envision IT!

Manifest IT!

ACTIVATE IT!

What's going to be your "go-to" word today?

"Success is not a mystery; so, let's make HERstory!" – Towandaism

Envision IT!

Manifest IT!

ACTIVATE IT!

What's going to be your "go-to" word today?

"Your conscious can either free you or enslave you; your conscious can effectively guide your risk-taking or shackle you to complacency; and your conscious can be divinely beautiful or devastatingly ugly...Entering via stage left, Choice! You are truly one decision away from a totally different life." – Towandaism

Envision IT!

Manifest IT!

ACTIVATE IT!

What's going to be your "go-to" word today?

"You can either read **HIStory** or make **HERstory**, the choice is yours!" – Towandaism

Envision IT!

Manifest IT!

ACTIVATE IT!

What's going to be your "go-to" word today?

"Just remember, a mind out of control will play interesting tricks on you; directed, it's your greatest and most invaluable asset!" – Towandaism

Envision IT!

Manifest IT!

ACTIVATE IT!

What's going to be your "go-to" word today?

"You are awesomely beautiful, talented and worthy! I pray you receive a tsunami of blessings and successes. Keep blocking negativity like a Boss; keep your eyes up towards God while your haters scramble under your feet!" – Towandaism

Envision IT!

Manifest IT!

ACTIVATE IT!

What's going to be your "go-to" word today?

"If you can't handle my SHINE, I suggest you buy some shades, because I will not be dimmed!"

– Towandaism

Envision IT!

Manifest IT!

ACTIVATE IT!

What's going to be your "go-to" word today?

"G.I.G is the acronym for Get It Goddess or Get It Girl, you choose!" – Towandaism

Envision IT!

Manifest IT!

ACTIVATE IT!

What's going to be your "go-to" word today?

"Live a life of:

Strength not shame;

Love not lies;

Prosperity not poverty;

Success not sin;

Happiness not hate;

Excellence not evil;

Joy not jealousy;

Awesomeness not anger; and

Respect not regrets." – Towandaism

Envision IT!

Manifest IT!

ACTIVATE IT!

What's going to be your "go-to" word today?

"Participate in your own Rescue and Participate in your own Success; both require that "dirty" word, WORK!" – Towandaism

Envision IT!

Manifest IT!

ACTIVATE IT!

What's going to be your "go-to" word today?

"You will be surprised at what happens when you stretch your wings." – Towandaism

Envision IT!

Manifest IT!

ACTIVATE IT!

What's going to be your "go-to" word today?

"It's your choice: The pain of Poverty or the pleasure of Prosperity; A life of lack or a life of light and luxury; and A peace of mind or dreams left in pieces. Choose well my friend." – Towandaism

Envision IT!

Manifest IT!

ACTIVATE IT!

What's going to be your "go-to" word today?

"Purposeful intentions must come with your passion to be of service to the world. The battles you are facing must be won in the spiritual realm in order for your blessings to be on flow. The Pouring Cycle, you pour yourself into people, your passion and the world; however, you must allow God to pour into you so your cup overflows abundantly which allows you to purposefully pour yourself into service unapologetically..."—Towandaism

Envision IT!

Manifest IT!

ACTIVATE IT!

What's going to be your "go-to" word today?

"Ask yourself what do I want out of this life? I promise you it will be trumped by what God wants for you!"

– Towandaism

Envision IT!

Manifest IT!

ACTIVATE IT!

What's going to be your "go-to" word today?

"Be every woman for one woman, YOU! Be every man for one man, YOU!" – Towandaism

Envision IT!

Manifest IT!

ACTIVATE IT!

What's going to be your "go-to" word today?

"Give yourself permission to be joyfully happy, overwhelmingly prosperous, and lavishly loved; then submit and commit yourself!" – Towandaism

Envision IT!

Manifest IT!

ACTIVATE IT!

What's going to be your "go-to" word today?

"Dreams don't come with expiration dates!" – Towandaism

Envision IT!

Manifest IT!

ACTIVATE IT!

What's going to be your "go-to" word today?

"They are not ready! Walk in your purpose, passion and possibilities..." – Towandaism

Envision IT!

Manifest IT!

ACTIVATE IT!

What's going to be your "go-to" word today?

"I wish I could tell you why I'm so determined to be successful and how I make the struggle look so damn sexy." – Towandaism

Envision IT!

Manifest IT!

ACTIVATE IT!

What's going to be your "go-to" word today?

"I've kissed the sun, danced on the moon and bathed in the stars; so, your "can'ts" and "won'ts" will never touch me; I am worthy, I am possible, I am woman." – Towandaism

Envision IT!

Manifest IT!

ACTIVATE IT!

What's going to be your "go-to" word today?

"Life and Love have shipwrecked me, abandoned me, deserted me, and tried to crush me; little did they know, I was built for this shit; so, here I stand stronger and braver than before; more beast than woman; and I dare you to try that shit again." – Towandaism

Envision IT!

Manifest IT!

ACTIVATE IT!

What's going to be your "go-to" word today?

"Step into your power, possibilities, purpose, passion, prosperity, and primeness." – Towandaism

Envision IT!

Manifest IT!

ACTIVATE IT!

What's going to be your "go-to" word today?

"Say to self, Get Off Your ASS and make Shit happen! WAIT! Know that you are worthy of immeasurably more!" – Towandaism

Envision IT!

Manifest IT!

ACTIVATE IT!

What's going to be your "go-to" word today?

"Success is the brand-new flavor in my ear!" – Towandaism

Envision IT!

Manifest IT!

ACTIVATE IT!

What's going to be your "go-to" word today?

"Why is it that we can handle the storm, but struggle when it drizzles? Why is it that we can handle the big rocks in our lives but trip over the pebbles? Why is it that we can navigate through a tsunami but fear the rippling waves? I'm just curious." – Towandaism

Envision IT!

Manifest IT!

ACTIVATE IT!

What's going to be your "go-to" word today?

"I'm in a tussle with fear and failure, no worries, I'm winning because I brought my friends faith and success." Towandaism

Envision IT!

Manifest IT!

ACTIVATE IT!

What's going to be your "go-to" word today?

"I have God's grace and grit so I will grind daily for not only the blessings I will see but those blessings I don't see." – Towandaism

Envision IT!

Manifest IT!

ACTIVATE IT!

What's going to be your "go-to" word today?

"STOP straddling and START striving for your goals, possibilities, purpose, passion and immeasurable success! Pursuing greatness requires WORK, put in the work NOW!" – Towandaism

Envision IT!

Manifest IT!

ACTIVATE IT!

What's going to be your "go-to" word today?

"There is only one way up and out, other than God; and that is Entrepreneurship! Lead, Follow or Get out the Way!" - Towandaism

Envision IT!

Manifest IT!

ACTIVATE IT!

What's going to be your "go-to" word today?

"The threat of leaving this world with my God given greatness untapped is pushing me towards my divine legacy..." – Towandaism

Envision IT!

Manifest IT!

ACTIVATE IT!

What's going to be your "go-to" word today?

"Folks want your glory but they are not built to live your story." – Towandaism

Envision IT!

Manifest IT!

ACTIVATE IT!

What's going to be your "go-to" word today?

"Thank you, Lord! I'm independently wealthy and financially secured! My business is thriving...Amen!"

– Towandaism

Envision IT!

Manifest IT!

ACTIVATE IT!

What's going to be your "go-to" word today?

"I'm a Divine Risk Taker, I don't see risks, I only see possibilities, because I'm a daughter of a God of possibilities." – Towandaism

Envision IT!

Manifest IT!

ACTIVATE IT!

What's going to be your "go-to" word today?

"If the eyes are windows to the soul; then I know you must see success, prosperity, purpose, passion and possibilities in mine." – Towandaism

Envision IT!

Manifest IT!

ACTIVATE IT!

What's going to be your "go-to" word today?

"Don't let your past discount your future...press forward, eyes forward, Vision forward, stay focused, blessings just ahead!" – Towandaism

Envision IT!

Manifest IT!

ACTIVATE IT!

What's going to be your "go-to" word today?

"The bottom of my shoes are **RED** because I'm crushing all of the competition...I possess the mind, body, soul and spirit of a **CHAMPION!**" – Towandaism

Envision IT!

Manifest IT!

ACTIVATE IT!

What's going to be your "go-to" word today?

"Make your next move your MOST BLESSED move!" – Towandaism

Envision IT!

Manifest IT!

ACTIVATE IT!

What's going to be your "go-to" word today?

"I was inspired, they laughed; I cried, they laughed; I stumbled, they laughed; I failed, they laughed; ahh SUCCESS, they are silent." – Towandaism

Envision IT!

Manifest IT!

ACTIVATE IT!

What's going to be your "go-to" word today?

"You are destined for a powerful, purposeful, positive flow of unbroken progress and prosperity...own it, work it and claim it." – Towandaism

Envision IT!

Manifest IT!

ACTIVATE IT!

What's going to be your "go-to" word today?

"My purpose as a servant leader is to show you how to prosper in any season e.g. during a winter storm, while others will struggle and be buried by avalanches; I would have prepared you to ski through Avalanches like a BOSS!" – Towandaism

Envision IT!

Manifest IT!

ACTIVATE IT!

What's going to be your "go-to" word today?

"Becoming a person of influence is what makes legends. Strive to become influential instead of famous, because fame is a fad and it will fade, it will go out of style (short term); however, if you become influential your impact will be eternal, generational and legendary." – Towandaism

Envision IT!

Manifest IT!

ACTIVATE IT!

What's going to be your "go-to" word today?

"My job/career is not my calling; it is the vehicle I'm using to fulfill my calling." – Towandaism

Envision IT!

Manifest IT!

ACTIVATE IT!

What's going to be your "go-to" word today?

"If you are afraid, you have taken your eyes off your goals."—Towandaism

Envision IT!

Manifest IT!

ACTIVATE IT!

What's going to be your "go-to" word today?

"No surrender…Success, you are mine!" – Towandaism

Envision IT!

Manifest IT!

ACTIVATE IT!

What's going to be your "go-to" word today?

"THE enemy will use weapons of mass-DISTRACTIONS to throw you off course and off purpose."
– Towandaism

Envision IT!

Manifest IT!

ACTIVATE IT!

What's going to be your "go-to" word today?

"Hey! Don't mix my Confidence with your arrogance! I know who I AM, take a good look this is what SUCCESS looks like." – Towandaism

Envision IT!

Manifest IT!

ACTIVATE IT!

What's going to be your "go-to" word today?

"When you have tasted the sweetness of Excellence it is hard to go back to being mediocre!" – Towandaism

Envision IT!

Manifest IT!

ACTIVATE IT!

What's going to be your "go-to" word today?

"I encourage you to walk in your purpose, serve selflessly, and ensure someone else's success that will guarantee yours!" – Towandaism

Envision IT!

Manifest IT!

ACTIVATE IT!

What's going to be your "go-to" word today?

"It is time to uproot and shake loose my blessings...!" – Towandaism

Envision IT!

Manifest IT!

ACTIVATE IT!

What's going to be your "go-to" word today?

"Today, let's give them something to talk about: I declare & decree scandalous successes and blessings for you today!" – Towandaism

Envision IT!

Manifest IT!

ACTIVATE IT!

What's going to be your "go-to" word today?

"Finish the statement.

I AM——!

everything that comes after these 2 words will manifest in your life." – Towandaism

Envision IT!

Manifest IT!

ACTIVATE IT!

What's going to be your "go-to" word today?

"I am worthy of my dreams, divine destinations and deliberate successes." — Towandaism

Envision IT!

Manifest IT!

ACTIVATE IT!

What's going to be your "go-to" word today?

"To live the life you always wanted, you have to have grit, you must grind and do all with grace."
– Towandaism

Envision IT!

Manifest IT!

ACTIVATE IT!

What's going to be your "go-to" word today?

"It's not the war zone or the rough journey to my purpose that scares me, because I've been in tougher fights than this; it's the suffering that comes with the crushing I must endure for my transformation that tries to test my faith and that has brought me to my knees; not in defeat but in prayer!" – Towandaism

Envision IT!

Manifest IT!

ACTIVATE IT!

What's going to be your "go-to" word today?

"Today is YOUR Transformation day so join me in slaying the 'the disease to please' and 'perfectionism'. Being a woman of excellence is not about being plastic perfect or killing yourself to be liked by everyone."
– Towandaism

Envision IT!

Manifest IT!

ACTIVATE IT!

What's going to be your "go-to" word today?

"YOU + GOD = UNSTOPPABLE!" – Towandaism

Envision IT!

Manifest IT!

ACTIVATE IT!

What's going to be your "go-to" word today?

"Loving yourself does not come with an expiration date; it does not matter what the world is saying about you, you my friend are **WORTHY!** Love yourself so much that it cures the ill-intentions of those that are hating on you!" – Towandaism

Envision IT!

Manifest IT!

ACTIVATE IT!

What's going to be your "go-to" word today?

"There will be days it may appear succeeding in this world is impossible, you may feel you don't have the complexion for the connection, the complexion of rejection, the gender that hinders...STOP IT! You are more than a CONQUEROR! You are a Champion, a Way-maker, and a Game-changer. The only thing that is impossible is failure when God is with you and in you!" – Towandaism

Envision IT!

Manifest IT!

ACTIVATE IT!

What's going to be your "go-to" word today?

"Sometimes you need more than a pat on your back, feel good words and prayers, a motivational talk, a good cry, and someone to tell you everything is going to be okay. Real talk, you just NEED someone to kick you in the ass, Tell you the truth about your bull stuff...REALITY CHECK PLEASE"

— Towandaism II

Envision IT!

Manifest IT!

ACTIVATE IT!

What's going to be your "go-to" word today?

"He asked me to describe myself in one word and I told him they haven't invented a word to describe me yet...but I'm working on it." – Towandaism

Envision IT!

Manifest IT!

ACTIVATE IT!

What's going to be your "go-to" word today?

"If you were waiting for a sign that it's time to make a change, that move or next step; ARISE CHAMPION, WAKE UP WARRIOR, THIS IS YOUR SIGN! Abundance, Prosperity, Success, Joy, Peace are screaming for your presence; answer the CALL!" – Towandaism

Envision IT!

Manifest IT!

ACTIVATE IT!

What's going to be your "go-to" word today?

Grit, Grind, & Grace -- ACTIVATE IT!

"I need you to stop what you are doing and receive this word; if you are complaining you are remaining; if you give praise you will be raised. My favored friend, you have your wings so you can't go back to old things...receive this word, plant this word, cultivate this word and make room for it grow and the fruit will be immeasurable." – Towandaism

Envision IT!

Manifest IT!

ACTIVATE IT!

What's going to be your "go-to" word today?

"She wore her brokenness like high fashion, she would not be drowned by the deadness in their eyes; determined to dream with boldness, stronger than the objections and rejections; She feared staying where she was more than where she was going; she claimed and owned her destiny. Now it's your turn!"

– Towandaism

Envision IT!

Manifest IT!

ACTIVATE IT!

What's going to be your "go-to" word today?

"They tried to bury her in their baggage, not being a baggage handler, she left that shit on the curb. Weightless she soared!" – Towandaism

Envision IT!

Manifest IT!

ACTIVATE IT!

What's going to be your "go-to" word today?

"Since I don't believe in New Year's resolutions, I decided to pick a word that would motivate me and my word this year is **MORE,** which is an acronym for Making Opportunities Rise Everywhere—and I continuously achieve that and **MORE!**" – Towandaism

Envision IT!

Manifest IT!

ACTIVATE IT!

What's going to be your "go-to" word today?

"Don't believe the lies of limitations! Abundance is yours! So, rejuvenate, replenish, refresh your soul through self-care to make room for the tsunami of successes you are about to receive...oh yeah, it is coming!" – Towandaism

Envision IT!

Manifest IT!

ACTIVATE IT!

What's going to be your "go-to" word today?

"Here's the deal I walk in my purpose daily! I take businesses from kitchens to killing it, from basements to bossing it and from garages to global! That's how I roll." – Towandaism

Envision IT!

Manifest IT!

ACTIVATE IT!

What's going to be your "go-to" word today?

"I was vs. I am; I used to be vs. I am called to be; I lived through vs. I am living for; I survived vs. I am thriving!" – Towandaism

Envision IT!

Manifest IT!

ACTIVATE IT!

What's going to be your "go-to" word today?

"Some days I really believe I can fly, so I do." – Towandaism

Envision IT!

Manifest IT!

ACTIVATE IT!

What's going to be your "go-to" word today?

"If you want to get warm you have to get close to the fire. Simply, if you want to be successful you must connect with others (fire) that are successful so that you can benefit and learn from them, so you can receive the spark you need to blaze a trail with your dreams; if you are the source of the fire, in order for you to have continuous success, you MUST bring warmth to others, so that, embers from your successes can ignite the passion and purpose in others; if you do your flame will be eternal and keep giving and growing people long after you have left this earth! So, are you the fire or are you seeking warmth?" – Towandaism

Envision IT!

Manifest IT!

ACTIVATE IT!

What's going to be your "go-to" word today?

"Believe In you! Believe in your goals and dreams! Believe in the impossible because you are a daughter/son of a Father that makes all things possible. Walk with expectation, Speak with expectation, Move with expectation, Live with expectation...make room for your overflow it has arrived!" – Towandaism

Envision IT!

Manifest IT!

ACTIVATE IT!

What's going to be your "go-to" word today?

"When you surround yourself with the right people, you can achieve the impossible!"
– Towandaism

Envision IT!

Manifest IT!

ACTIVATE IT!

What's going to be your "go-to" word today?

"I have slayed many Goliaths, checked the boneyard I have left behind, no I'm not a bone collector, my handbags are not made to carry bones. I'm bruised and not broken; bring it on and you will be buried in the boneyard I have tossed and slayed many Goliaths!" – Towandaism

Envision IT!

Manifest IT!

ACTIVATE IT!

What's going to be your "go-to" word today?

"You want to change your life? Change your "I am!" – Towandaism

Envision IT!

Manifest IT!

ACTIVATE IT!

What's going to be your "go-to" word today?

"Let's be clear, I'm PRO-Wealth; I'm just ANTI-Greed, ANTI-Gluttony, ANTI-the worship of the false idol of money!" – Towandaism

Envision IT!

Manifest IT!

ACTIVATE IT!

What's going to be your "go-to" word today?

"You were waiting for a divine sign HERE IT ITS!!!- Build it! Rebuild it! Keep Going! Restore it! Rejuvenate it! Keep climbing! Dream it, Design it and Do it! Redeem it! Claim it and Reclaim it! The time is NOW! May God find you where you need to be!" – Towandaism

Envision IT!

Manifest IT!

ACTIVATE IT!

What's going to be your "go-to" word today?

"Don't be a victim of your choices; become the director of your destiny! You are victorious!"
– Towandaism

Envision IT!

Manifest IT!

ACTIVATE IT!

What's going to be your "go-to" word today?

"Life is not about the accumulation of material things...I have never seen a U-Haul or BRINKS truck following a hearse. Live a life filled with gratitude and service no Black Friday discounts required for access to Heaven." – Towandaism

Envision IT!

Manifest IT!

ACTIVATE IT!

What's going to be your "go-to" word today?

Grind - Spadework

"I must make it to the Top of Business, Life and Service because the bottom is too overcrowded."

– Towandaism

Envision IT!

Manifest IT!

ACTIVATE IT!

What's going to be your "go-to" word today?

Rise and Shine, Success Maven! Girl, pray, re-evaluate and clean up your circle, get your mind right so your grind will earn you money in your sleep, get up and level up—your dreams have been waiting and they are shouting "you are late girl!" So, get to claiming your prosperity and immeasurable blessings!"

– Towandaism

Envision IT!

Manifest IT!

ACTIVATE IT!

What's going to be your "go-to" word today?

"Have you placed the responsibility of your miracle or success in the hands of others? Have you delegated what you have been anointed for to others? If it is your purpose, vision, or mission, you must take hold of it, lead it and do the spade work. It's yours, so OWN IT!" – Towandaism

Envision IT!

Manifest IT!

ACTIVATE IT!

What's going to be your "go-to" word today?

"I'm not a pebble skipping across a pond and making ripples, I'm a mountain falling into an ocean causing a tsunami..." – Towandaism

Envision IT!

Manifest IT!

ACTIVATE IT!

What's going to be your "go-to" word today?

"I need to make room for my money to multiple immeasurably, continuously and generationally."
– Towandaism

Envision IT!

Manifest IT!

ACTIVATE IT!

What's going to be your "go-to" word today?

"Unfortunately, there are little people in big positions; and building on that misfortune we keep little people in key roles too long...little people with little minds can't dream, lead, aspire, inspire, motivate; little people with little minds can't show compassion, kindness and generosity. Little people with little minds have no self-control and make emotional and irrational decisions without regard to consequences. Little people with little minds will be our undoing, unless we speak up, stand up and get fed up and take action."

– Towandaism

Envision IT!

Manifest IT!

ACTIVATE IT!

What's going to be your "go-to" word today?

Ignorance = Poverty + Pain

Ignorance - Access = Systematic Poverty + Oppressive Pain

Knowledge + Access = Limitless Success + Continuous Pleasure

Get it, Got it, Good...now ACT!" – Towandaism

Envision IT!

Manifest IT!

ACTIVATE IT!

What's going to be your "go-to" word today?

"When a car goes up a hill, it shifts into a different gear to get over the hill and to gain more climbing power and speed. I need you to shift into that gear today! Some of you have hills or mountains to get over in your life that requires you to shift into a different gear to get over. You have someplace to be; your prosperity, success, health, wealth, peace of mind, and freedom is just over the hill; so, today, commit to shifting into unstoppable mode." – Towandaism

Envision IT!

Manifest IT!

ACTIVATE IT!

What's going to be your "go-to" word today?

"Evolution requires revolution - you must resolve to evolve - you must be so sick and tired, fed up and downright disgusted at where you are, that you incite a riot within yourself to push you into your greatness!" – Towandaism

Envision IT!

Manifest IT!

ACTIVATE IT!

What's going to be your "go-to" word today?

"When death catches me, I pray it finds me scaling a new mountain instead of sliding down an old one! Failing forward, because I'm future-focused!" – Towandaism

Envision IT!

Manifest IT!

ACTIVATE IT!

What's going to be your "go-to" word today?

"You need folks in your circle of influence that have your back and see you through, not until the battle is done, but until the battle is won." – Towandaism

Envision IT!

Manifest IT!

ACTIVATE IT!

What's going to be your "go-to" word today?

Repeat after me — "This is my year to turn it around, turn it up and turn it out!" – Towandaism

Envision IT!

Manifest IT!

ACTIVATE IT!

What's going to be your "go-to" word today?

"Rise and Shine Queen! Today you will dare to dream, divinely dominate and devastatingly destroy your enemies. Girl, live boldly with your bad self!" – Towandaism

Envision IT!

Manifest IT!

ACTIVATE IT!

What's going to be your "go-to" word today?

"Plot Twist! Be a Jane/Jack-of-all trades and a Master of One! (*Folks love a one-stop shop.*) You can do anything, but not everything (*at the same time*). Absolutely, you can do a lot of things very well, just make sure you're at least excellent at one thing, intentionally; and make sure all things you are working on or whatever has your attention, feeds your purpose, passion and limitless possibilities." – Towandaism

Envision IT!

Manifest IT!

ACTIVATE IT!

What's going to be your "go-to" word today?

"Privilege will never trump pain, purpose and possibilities. The color of your skin, your gender, the amount of money in your bank account, and how many people of influence you know doesn't matter. You will never escape the pains of life, suffering and death; you will never lessen the possibilities of those with less than you have; and you will **NEVER** defeat a person with **PURPOSE!** The price of privilege is service; until you learn to serve more, give more and do more for others; all of your gains will serve to generationally destroy you." – Towandaism

Envision IT!

Manifest IT!

ACTIVATE IT!

What's going to be your "go-to" word today?

"Money is a good servant, but a poor master; money is a good passenger, but not a great driver; money buys, but God provides." – Towandaism

Envision IT!

Manifest IT!

ACTIVATE IT!

What's going to be your "go-to" word today?

"While your enemies are digging graves for your purpose, passions and possibilities; God is building stages to exalt you, to elevate you and illuminate you. You will dominate this year; and, everything you lay your hands on will flourish, prosper and multiply to God's glory and for your good."

– Towandaism

Envision IT!

Manifest IT!

ACTIVATE IT!

What's going to be your "go-to" word today?

"A person who is committed will outpace, overcome and outperform a person with talent always!"

– Towandaism

Envision IT!

Manifest IT!

ACTIVATE IT!

What's going to be your "go-to" word today?

"The struggle is guaranteed, success is not; so, Rise, Shine, Grind, and Dominate, gracefully! – Towandaism

Envision IT!

Manifest IT!

ACTIVATE IT!

What's going to be your "go-to" word today?

"Our world is materially blessed and spiritually lost." – Towandaism

Envision IT!

Manifest IT!

ACTIVATE IT!

What's going to be your "go-to" word today?

"You have allowed your focus to be arrested by your current crisis. There will always be suffering before success, so, dust yourself off and get back on the pathway to your purpose." – Towandaism

Envision IT!

Manifest IT!

ACTIVATE IT!

What's going to be your "go-to" word today?

"In business, as in life, purposeful planning is critical and taking action is not optional. ACTIVATE NOW! Give your dreams strong legs that will carry you to your destiny." – Towandaism

Envision IT!

Manifest IT!

ACTIVATE IT!

What's going to be your "go-to" word today?

"When you think about quitting. Remember, your success is not just about you, it's also about the folks that have helped you along your journey; and those who are waiting for you to show up so they can fulfill their purposes." – Towandaism

Envision IT!

Manifest IT!

ACTIVATE IT!

What's going to be your "go-to" word today?

"There will be struggle before your SHINE! So, buckle up, rise up, claim it and Shine On!" – Towandaism

Envision IT!

Manifest IT!

ACTIVATE IT!

What's going to be your "go-to" word today?

"What if in Business we viewed our bottom-line as a pipeline that divinely serves people in ways that ensures their prosperity; instead of having a bottom-line that's a slave to profits? Now that's wealth building!" – Towandaism

Envision IT!

Manifest IT!

ACTIVATE IT!

What's going to be your "go-to" word today?

"I need you to **STOP** what you doing and put your hand over your heart; feel that? That's **PURPOSE**! Keep going!" – Towandaism

Envision IT!

Manifest IT!

ACTIVATE IT!

What's going to be your "go-to" word today?

"Don't let the mediocre standards of others cap your infinite possibilities." –
Towandaism

Envision IT!

Manifest IT!

ACTIVATE IT!

What's going to be your "go-to" word today?

"Don't confuse needs with greeds; there are legitimate and noble ways to satisfy your needs and to help you thrive; however, greeds are insatiable and require constant feeding. Greeds don't care about others or the methods or means; and, this insatiable hunger will lead you down paths of self-destruction, isolation and irrelevancy." – Towandaism

Envision IT!

Manifest IT!

ACTIVATE IT!

What's going to be your "go-to" word today?

"I shed my poverty thinking and I was reborn a Champion among men and a Warrior among women...I eat, live, breathe Excellence." – Towandaism

Envision IT!

Manifest IT!

ACTIVATE IT!

What's going to be your "go-to" word today?

"No! You can't have your dreams, purposes, visions or successes on credit. Your credit isn't that good! You MUST put in the spade work. If you don't do the work, expect discounted dreams, purposes, visions and successes; EXPECT to live a life less than what you were created to live." – Towandaism

Envision IT!

Manifest IT!

ACTIVATE IT!

What's going to be your "go-to" word today?

"The difference between successful people and unsuccessful people, champions and losers, wealthy people and poor people, people of excellence and those that settle on being mediocre…it is what they do during the PAUSE; they keep praying and pushing forward during the PAUSE, while others second guess themselves and "dirty talk" themselves out of pursuing the possibilities during the PAUSE. STOP "dirty talking" yourselves during the pauses in life and work and press on to your best and most blessed YOU!"

– Towandaism

Envision IT!

Manifest IT!

ACTIVATE IT!

What's going to be your "go-to" word today?

"Just like Jacob wrestled with the archangel until he blessed him; I need you to wrestle with life and the universe until it delivers ALL that has been earmarked for you! Don't dare give up! Yes, you might walk away with a limp like Jacob, but I promise you it will be worth it! Besides it is better to walk through life with a limp and blessed immeasurably, than to be whole in body and poor in mind, spirit, soul, finances, blessings, possibilities, purpose and passion." – Towandaism

Envision IT!

Manifest IT!

ACTIVATE IT!

What's going to be your "go-to" word today?

"My Friends, I would strongly encourage you to find the crowns in the crosses, the palaces in the prisons, and the sovereignty in the suffering." – Towandaism

Envision IT!

Manifest IT!

ACTIVATE IT!

What's going to be your "go-to" word today?

"We will all thrive once we realize, we are all mutually dependent on each other for not only our survival but our success!" – Towandaism

Envision IT!

Manifest IT!

ACTIVATE IT!

What's going to be your "go-to" word today?

"I need you to put down that wishbone and get a backbone! When you fall, GET UP! When you're sick, GET UP! When you are depressed, GET UP, GET DRESS, MOVE…yes, it will be hard but WORTH it! Don't let this moment, this lesson, this relationship, this job, this illness be your burial ground, make it your stomping ground to grow and strengthen your emotional and spiritual muscles!" – Towandaism

Envision IT!

Manifest IT!

ACTIVATE IT!

What's going to be your "go-to" word today?

"Some of you are watering rocks that will never bear fruit; and some of you are watering seeds that will bear immeasurable fruit." – Towandaism

Envision IT!

Manifest IT!

ACTIVATE IT!

What's going to be your "go-to" word today?

"In order to live successfully you have to have book-sense, common-sense, and street-sense to increase your dollars and cents!" – Towandaism

Envision IT!

Manifest IT!

ACTIVATE IT!

What's going to be your "go-to" word today?

"I have shifted my thought and attitude patterns to a queendom paradigm. I've crushed all negativity, poverty pushers, time and joy stealers with my red glass stilettos. My queendom paradigm only focuses on ensuring good health, creating & sustaining great wealth and pursuing my God-given passion, purpose and possibilities with a ferocious appetite!" – Towandaism

Envision IT!

Manifest IT!

ACTIVATE IT!

What's going to be your "go-to" word today?

"God is asking you, 'are you done yet?' You keep trying to do it your way and with your plans and keep coming up short. So, are you done yet?" – Towandaism

Envision IT!

Manifest IT!

ACTIVATE IT!

What's going to be your "go-to" word today?

"Sometimes there is more Month than Money; nonetheless God always provides abundantly and generously. I'm declaring and decreeing that you will be independently wealthy and financially secure."

– Towandaism

Envision IT!

Manifest IT!

ACTIVATE IT!

What's going to be your "go-to" word today?

"Your limitations are my starting line, I was not born to be mediocre, I was born to be a Champion!"
– Towandaism

Envision IT!

Manifest IT!

ACTIVATE IT!

What's going to be your "go-to" word today?

"In order to succeed and achieve immeasurable greatness YOU must 'doubt your doubts and believe your beliefs,' without ceasing!" – Towandaism

Envision IT!

Manifest IT!

ACTIVATE IT!

What's going to be your "go-to" word today?

"Stop hosting Pity Parties and getting mad when some folks RSVP (*Hating Hattie, Negative Nancy, Pessimistic Polly, and Doubting Debbie*); instead Host Success Sessions, Excellence Escapades, Cash Conferences, Get it Girl Gatherings, and Awaken Assemblies!" – Towandaism

Envision IT!

Manifest IT!

ACTIVATE IT!

What's going to be your "go-to" word today?

"You can't casually stroll into success, greatness, your purpose or possibilities; YOU MUST RUN TO IT! I don't care if my lungs collapse, I'm going to leave it ALL on this Track called Life! I'm coming for all that God has promised me and if you are not with me, get out my way, stop the negativity and take your seat in the stadium, you spectator; this is a grown-ass woman race!" – Towandaism

Envision IT!

Manifest IT!

ACTIVATE IT!

What's going to be your "go-to" word today?

"Don't be a History Teacher, be a History-maker! Be Forward-focused and Future-focused! Always onward and upward! Stop watering dead plants!" – Towandaism

Envision IT!

Manifest IT!

ACTIVATE IT!

What's going to be your "go-to" word today?

"Ships are safe in the harbor, but that is not what they are built for. So, what blessings are you blocking because you are playing it safe?" – Towandaism

Envision IT!

Manifest IT!

ACTIVATE IT!

What's going to be your "go-to" word today?

"Say to self, Get Off MY ASS and make Shit happen! WAIT! Know that you are worthy of immeasurably more!" – Towandaism

Envision IT!

Manifest IT!

ACTIVATE IT!

What's going to be your "go-to" word today?

"I'm often asked what makes a great public speaker or presenter, and my answer is always the same, AUTHENTICITY! Once you step up to the microphone it stops being about you, it's ALL about the audience. Ask yourself prior to your presentation/speech, what is the most valuable thing "they" want from me, who are they, what are their needs, and what is one precious gem I could share with them that will elevate their hustle?" – Towandaism

Envision IT!

Manifest IT!

ACTIVATE IT!

What's going to be your "go-to" word today?

"I refuse to stand in my past, what I "used to be"; I must stand firmly in God's word, my divine purpose, passion and possibilities. I will stand ON my story, but I refuse to wallow in my story, because I don't water dead plants! My past is the foundation God used to build my emotional muscle, humility, competency, confidence, heart, capabilities, capacity, servitude, leadership etc... THANK YOU, GOD!" – Towandaism

Envision IT!

Manifest IT!

ACTIVATE IT!

What's going to be your "go-to" word today?

"Disrupting the Norm - men are hired, promoted, advanced or giving opportunities based on their Potential and women based on their PERFORMANCE- you have the POWER to DISRUPT the norm, so do it!"

– Towandaism

Envision IT!

Manifest IT!

ACTIVATE IT!

What's going to be your "go-to" word today?

"Here's what I know for sure—they don't sell confidence, courage, and commitment at the convenience store. Daily, you must work at increasing your confidence, courage and commitment levels." – Towandaism

Envision IT!

Manifest IT!

ACTIVATE IT!

What's going to be your "go-to" word today?

"While you are playing someone else is planning. While you are playing someone else is praying. While you are getting played someone else is getting paid!" – Towandaism

Envision IT!

Manifest IT!

ACTIVATE IT!

What's going to be your "go-to" word today?

"Fact! The cheapest commodity on earth is advice. So, take care who you receive advice from; guard your mind, body, soul, business, family, and marriage from ill-advised and unwise counsel." – Towandaism

Envision IT!

Manifest IT!

ACTIVATE IT!

What's going to be your "go-to" word today?

"Read the small print under SUCCESS, it states, Spadework required." – Towandaism

Envision IT!

Manifest IT!

ACTIVATE IT!

What's going to be your "go-to" word today?

"You are closing deals in heels and your blessings are on FLOW!" – Towandaism

Envision IT!

Manifest IT!

ACTIVATE IT!

What's going to be your "go-to" word today?

"I refuse to carry into my present and future, the past, the old and the dead; let the dead bury the dead! I'm packing light, love, prosperity, excellence, success, servitude and gratitude for my journey. See, where I'm headed, darkness and negativity cannot exist!" – Towandaism

Envision IT!

Manifest IT!

ACTIVATE IT!

What's going to be your "go-to" word today?

"As a successful person or entrepreneur, you MUST consistently, make money, manage money and multiple money. Yes, a fool and his money is soon parted; however, a financially independent and savvy woman attracts and sustains multiple revenue streams and her pockets and accounts overflow with abundance."
– Towandaism

Envision IT!

Manifest IT!

ACTIVATE IT!

What's going to be your "go-to" word today?

"Today, make MOVES that matter!" – Towandaism

Envision IT!

Manifest IT!

ACTIVATE IT!

What's going to be your "go-to" word today?

"God's rejection is his protection while he gives you and your purpose direction." –
Towandaism

Envision IT!

Manifest IT!

ACTIVATE IT!

What's going to be your "go-to" word today?

"Those that doubted you and betted against you, better get ready for a refund!" – Towandaism

Envision IT!

Manifest IT!

ACTIVATE IT!

What's going to be your "go-to" word today?

"Get your house in order - stop being raggedy, reckless, ratchet and wretched - just because life has knocked you down to beneath the bottom it is not permission to give up...ARISE Champion!" – Towandaism

Envision IT!

Manifest IT!

ACTIVATE IT!

What's going to be your "go-to" word today?

"Yes, you can lack goals, be lazy, let your dreams remain wishes, do a 9 to 5 and eke out a living, be constantly in a survival mode; there is a name for you, EMPLOYEE! Unleash your entrepreneurial beast TODAY!" – Towandaism

Envision IT!

Manifest IT!

ACTIVATE IT!

What's going to be your "go-to" word today?

"In order to achieve sustainable success, the pain of poverty, being broke and broken has to be so excruciating that it forces you to keep leveling up." – Towandaism

Envision IT!

Manifest IT!

ACTIVATE IT!

What's going to be your "go-to" word today?

"Making deals in heels, increasing my bottom-line without raising my hemline; my blessings are on an endless *FLOW!*" – Towandaism

Envision IT!

Manifest IT!

ACTIVATE IT!

What's going to be your "go-to" word today?

"The good thing is that she showed you who she is, so now you know how to deal with her...aging doesn't increase knowledge or intelligence, some folks are stuck, just don't let them pull you in their quick sand."
– Towandaism

Envision IT!

Manifest IT!

ACTIVATE IT!

What's going to be your "go-to" word today?

"The ultimate luxury gift you can give someone is your time, because you will never get it back."

– Towandaism

Envision IT!

Manifest IT!

ACTIVATE IT!

What's going to be your "go-to" word today?

"You are not the only victim of you not walking in your purpose, passion and possibilities; the other casualties are the folks whose dreams are deferred by your inaction." – Towandaism

Envision IT!

Manifest IT!

ACTIVATE IT!

What's going to be your "go-to" word today?

"When lightning attempts to strike your family, health, career, finances or opportunities become a lightning rod!" – Towandaism

Envision IT!

Manifest IT!

ACTIVATE IT!

What's going to be your "go-to" word today?

"You do your spadework by your means; and watch God do the rest by supernatural means...God wants us to put in the work so he can show up great for us!" – Towandaism

Envision IT!

Manifest IT!

ACTIVATE IT!

What's going to be your "go-to" word today?

"I failed my way to success." – Towandaism

Envision IT!

Manifest IT!

ACTIVATE IT!

What's going to be your "go-to" word today?

"To ACHIEVE anything in Life, you must say to yourself constantly & daily: I SPEAK IT, I BELIEVE IT, I RECEIVE IT! You must CLAIM your WINS daily!" – Towandaism

Envision IT!

Manifest IT!

ACTIVATE IT!

What's going to be your "go-to" word today?

"If you want to live like a Queen, you must do a Queen's worth of work. If you want to live like a King, you must do a King's worth of work." – Towandaism

Envision IT!

Manifest IT!

ACTIVATE IT!

What's going to be your "go-to" word today?

"Entrepreneurs or 'Futurepreneurs,' Don't buy yourself another job; instead, invest in your DREAMS!"
– Towandaism

Envision IT!

Manifest IT!

ACTIVATE IT!

What's going to be your "go-to" word today?

"Yes, I needed this dose of reality; and **ABSOLUTELY**, the push of my purpose has become greater than the comfort of my complacency." – Towandaism

Envision IT!

Manifest IT!

ACTIVATE IT!

What's going to be your "go-to" word today?

"Success is not convenient and failure is not an option!" – Towandaism

Envision IT!

Manifest IT!

ACTIVATE IT!

What's going to be your "go-to" word today?

"I don't just hunger for success; I'm starving for it and it is in this starvation mode I'm pushed into my purpose." – Towandaism

Envision IT!

Manifest IT!

ACTIVATE IT!

What's going to be your "go-to" word today?

"In life as in business you either have to demonstrate or starve. The choice is yours!"
– Towandaism

Envision IT!

Manifest IT!

ACTIVATE IT!

What's going to be your "go-to" word today?

"Tell them, better yet, show them WINNING is your protocol!" – Towandaism

Envision IT!

Manifest IT!

ACTIVATE IT!

What's going to be your "go-to" word today?

"Problems are simply opportunities in work clothes." – Henry J. Kaiser - "Those work clothes are sometimes the grimmest, smelliest and tattered overalls, hard hats and work boots you have ever worn; however, the opportunities are worth it!" – Towandaism

Envision IT!

Manifest IT!

ACTIVATE IT!

What's going to be your "go-to" word today?

"It is simple, improving your IQ + EQ + AQ will increase your Success, Prosperity & Peace of Mind! IQ= Intelligence Quotient, EQ=Emotional Quotient, AQ=Adaptability Quotient" – Towandaism

Envision IT!

Manifest IT!

ACTIVATE IT!

What's going to be your "go-to" word today?

"I'm sorry being poor just don't look good on me; dress by Excellence, shoes by Success; now I wear them well." – Towandaism

Envision IT!

Manifest IT!

ACTIVATE IT!

What's going to be your "go-to" word today?

"Take the parking brakes on your life, career, prosperity off (I know it's comfortable, however comfort does not produce success.) and shift them into overdrive, FULL throttle; ride them until the wheels fall off!"

– Towandaism

Envision IT!

Manifest IT!

ACTIVATE IT!

What's going to be your "go-to" word today?

"Complacency equates to death, I'm a daughter of the living God, living King...I walk by him...I have faith he has ordered my steps and words." – Towandaism

Envision IT!

Manifest IT!

ACTIVATE IT!

What's going to be your "go-to" word today?

"Why do folks want success, wealth and a life of abundance before they put in the sweat equity required to earn these things? That's like sitting in front of an oven and saying give me heat and then I'll put in the fuel! Grind, the blessings will flow." – Towandaism

Envision IT!

Manifest IT!

ACTIVATE IT!

What's going to be your "go-to" word today?

"If you haven't received your breakthrough consider that it might be the environment. See weeds can grow anywhere, however lilies, roses and orchids require fertile soil and a nurturing environment; stop clinging to barren land and break free from negative environments. God will not release your tsunami of blessings until you free yourself from your toxic environment." – Towandaism

Envision IT!

Manifest IT!

ACTIVATE IT!

What's going to be your "go-to" word today?

"Failures are what give your success story flavor!" – Towandaism

Envision IT!

Manifest IT!

ACTIVATE IT!

What's going to be your "go-to" word today?

"Stop being so damn comfortable with being Good and pursue GREATNESS! Stop settling for Average and be AWESOME!" – Towandaism

Envision IT!

Manifest IT!

ACTIVATE IT!

What's going to be your "go-to" word today?

"I eat FEAR for breakfast and I walk, run, no soar in FAITH boldly!" – Towandaism

Envision IT!

Manifest IT!

ACTIVATE IT!

What's going to be your "go-to" word today?

"It takes brains to run a business but it takes estrogen to start one!" – Towandaism

Envision IT!

Manifest IT!

ACTIVATE IT!

What's going to be your "go-to" word today?

"I continue to walk in God's favor, victory and glory not just on my behalf, but on the behalf of the people he has put me on the path to serve with excellence. I am a **CHAMPION** among men and a **WARRIOR** among women and **SO ARE YOU!**" – Towandaism

Envision IT!

Manifest IT!

ACTIVATE IT!

What's going to be your "go-to" word today?

"The beaten path is kryptonite to me; I was created to forge new paths to serve those that need a roadmap to their destiny." – Towandaism

Envision IT!

Manifest IT!

ACTIVATE IT!

What's going to be your "go-to" word today?

"On the other side of discipline and determination is My Destiny!" – Towandaism

Envision IT!

Manifest IT!

ACTIVATE IT!

What's going to be your "go-to" word today?

"I was built for success and prosperity; my time is now...I got my faith shoes on and I'm strutting into my blessings." – Towandaism

Envision IT!

Manifest IT!

ACTIVATE IT!

What's going to be your "go-to" word today?

"It is time to SHINE, SPARKLE, GLOW...please take a moment to realize how powerful the light is inside of you; you have been holding back in 2017; Now it's 2018, 2019, 2020, 2021 it is time to unleash the SHINE! It's your winning season, you MUST Shine so bright that your haters will need shades. I refuse to let you settle on being someone's shadow when my sweet dear you are the SUBSTANCE!" – Towandaism

Envision IT!

Manifest IT!

ACTIVATE IT!

What's going to be your "go-to" word today?

"Don't let the mediocre standards of others cap your infinite possibilities." – Towandaism

Envision IT!

Manifest IT!

ACTIVATE IT!

What's going to be your "go-to" word today?

"There is a drum that beats deep inside of you, if you silence yourself you can hear the beat, no it is not your heartbeat, it's a warrior's tune, it's a warrior's soul, it's a warrior's spirit, and it is this warrior drum song that thumps healing, victory, peace, love, prosperity, hope, blessings in you, for you and through you. This is the drum I need you to dance to daily." – Towandaism

Envision IT!

Manifest IT!

ACTIVATE IT!

What's going to be your "go-to" word today?

"I pinky swear, I'm coming for all that has been promised to me by my Father, a great King!"
– Towandaism

Envision IT!

Manifest IT!

ACTIVATE IT!

What's going to be your "go-to" word today?

"People want the conveniences of success; however, they do not want the inconveniences of the hard work that is required to be successful." – Towandaism

Envision IT!

Manifest IT!

ACTIVATE IT!

What's going to be your "go-to" word today?

"I don't show up for the crowds, it's about the crowns, I told you I'm coming for ALL that God promised, so I'm claiming all crowns: grace, mercy, prosperity, favor, abundance, victory, success, love etc."
– Towandaism

Envision IT!

Manifest IT!

ACTIVATE IT!

What's going to be your "go-to" word today?

I'm a predator and my prey are peace, success, and prosperity; and I'm hungry!" – Towandaism

Envision IT!

Manifest IT!

ACTIVATE IT!

What's going to be your "go-to" word today?

"I'm making room for success, planning for prosperity, and activating my abundance flow." – Towandaism

Envision IT!

Manifest IT!

ACTIVATE IT!

What's going to be your "go-to" word today?

"For years I thought that I had to leave it all on the field when pursuing sustainable success; I did this at the expense of my health...taking time for me was not an option for me. Now I know that I have to redefine being a warrior among women and a champion among men; the first step is self-care!" – Towandaism

Envision IT!

Manifest IT!

ACTIVATE IT!

What's going to be your "go-to" word today?

"The choice IS yours; you can be a Host to Faith or hostage to your fears." – Towandaism

Envision IT!

Manifest IT!

ACTIVATE IT!

What's going to be your "go-to" word today?

"The greatest Goliath you will ever face is within you." – Towandaism

Envision IT!

Manifest IT!

ACTIVATE IT!

What's going to be your "go-to" word today?

"Build it! Build your business, Build your finances, Build your family, Build your blessings, Build your confidence, Build your network, Build your home, Build your faith, Build your joy, Build your career, Build strength, Build courage...A wise woman Builds!" – Towandaism

Envision IT!

Manifest IT!

ACTIVATE IT!

What's going to be your "go-to" word today?

"Do you play to WIN or play not to lose? Your answer to this question will determine whether you will achieve sustainable SUCCESS!" – Towandaism

Envision IT!

Manifest IT!

ACTIVATE IT!

What's going to be your "go-to" word today?

"I may get there first, but I will not get there by myself and I won't be alone." –
Towandaism

Envision IT!

Manifest IT!

ACTIVATE IT!

What's going to be your "go-to" word today?

"Be a success savage!" – Towandaism

Envision IT!

Manifest IT!

ACTIVATE IT!

What's going to be your "go-to" word today?

"Increasing the one-percenters daily and committed to moving those from the bottom of the economic ladder to over crowd the one-percenters...in fact, I'm building an elevator to the top!" – Towandaism

Envision IT!

Manifest IT!

ACTIVATE IT!

What's going to be your "go-to" word today?

"Quiet the noise in your head of what others have told you who you should be or who you will never be; turn up the volume of your authentic voice, so you can live a life filled with purpose, passion and limitless possibilities." – Towandaism

Envision IT!

Manifest IT!

ACTIVATE IT!

What's going to be your "go-to" word today?

"Nothing less than **EXCELLENCE** & always more..." – Towandaism

Envision IT!

Manifest IT!

ACTIVATE IT!

What's going to be your "go-to" word today?

"Big girls don't cry, they multiply; big girls don't fail they sail; big girls don't concede, they lead; big girls don't troll, they stroll; big girls don't shove, they love; big girls don't hate, they have faith; big girls don't stop until they reach the top!" – Towandaism

Envision IT!

Manifest IT!

ACTIVATE IT!

What's going to be your "go-to" word today?

"The **COMEBACK** is always more memorable than a setback; I love it when the comeback smiles and winks at those who thought they had won during the setback!" – Towandaism

Envision IT!

Manifest IT!

ACTIVATE IT!

What's going to be your "go-to" word today?

"The following can't live in the same heart, share the same space or travel the same journey, you must choose: conviction or convenience; courage or comfort; bad ass or slacker; and faith or fear!"

– Towandaism

Envision IT!

Manifest IT!

ACTIVATE IT!

What's going to be your "go-to" word today?

"Who I am today is far less than who I will be tomorrow!" – Towandaism

Envision IT!

Manifest IT!

ACTIVATE IT!

What's going to be your "go-to" word today?

"What I know for sure: Change is inevitable, not impossible. Being able to adapt quickly and efficiently to an ever-changing environment is paramount to your SUCCESS in life, business and the workplace. *Famous Chinese proverb states, "When the winds of change blow, some people build walls and others build windmills."* It is my hope that, every day of your life, YOU build fields of WINDMILLS." – Towandaism

Envision IT!

Manifest IT!

ACTIVATE IT!

What's going to be your "go-to" word today?

"Hey there! Just wanted you to know that WINNING looks good on YOU! Keep it up!" – Towandaism

Envision IT!

Manifest IT!

ACTIVATE IT!

What's going to be your "go-to" word today?

"Get real with yourself! Stop the false humility and stop using your faith as a crutch or free pass to fuck shit up! Own your shit, stop playing the martyr and get your ass in gear! Get your mind, body, soul, spirit, house, finances, career, family and business in divine order. Make room for God to show up GREAT in your life!" – Towandaism

Envision IT!

Manifest IT!

ACTIVATE IT!

What's going to be your "go-to" word today?

"You must violate human rules to take hold of what God has anointed for you! Faith is an action word, so take hold of what has been ordained for you! Claim it NOW!" – Towandaism

Envision IT!

Manifest IT!

ACTIVATE IT!

What's going to be your "go-to" word today?

"Bankrupt It!!! Bankrupt depression, bankrupt divorce, bankrupt self-hate, bankrupt self-sabotage, bankrupt the "I can'ts," bankrupt poverty, bankrupt unemployment, bankrupt debt, bankrupt complacency, bankrupt conformity, bankrupt procrastination, bankrupt mass distractions, bankrupt promiscuity, bankrupt every sin, addiction, bad habit and proclivity!!! You are now FREE! Every chain broken! Thank God, you are FREE!" – Towandaism

Envision IT!

Manifest IT!

ACTIVATE IT!

What's going to be your "go-to" word today?

"Stop confusing being educated with having wisdom—you can have numerous degrees and guess what, continuous failures and self-sabotaging behaviors will find you. Wisdom is a mindset, Wealth is a mindset, Success is a mindset and Excellence is a mindset. Change your mindset, you will change your life!"
– Towandaism

Envision IT!

Manifest IT!

ACTIVATE IT!

What's going to be your "go-to" word today?

"Pain or Purpose? What's tugging at you? What's pushing you? May it be the pain of not walking in your purpose that pushes you to greatness!" – Towandaism

Envision IT!

Manifest IT!

ACTIVATE IT!

What's going to be your "go-to" word today?

"Friday Mood -- Friday Flow is on beast mode, yes, I make it look easy, that's what lionesses do!"

– Towandaism

Envision IT!

Manifest IT!

ACTIVATE IT!

What's going to be your "go-to" word today?

"Here's the deal...life and work will throw so much shit at you it will cause you to rationalize (which stands for "ration-lies") why you can't achieve your dreams; because of the inconveniences of success? Don't give yourself the opportunity...so many have sold their dreams and successes for conveniences...Do the Spadework! – Towandaism

Envision IT!

Manifest IT!

ACTIVATE IT!

What's going to be your "go-to" word today?

"If you are living on a 100% of your income - I decree and declare a favorable change in your finances is upon you, it requires you to commit to change **TODAY**, commit to a wealth mindset. No shame! No blame! Give yourself permission to be debt free, to be prosperous and to become independently wealthy and financially secure." – Towandaism

Envision IT!

Manifest IT!

ACTIVATE IT!

What's going to be your "go-to" word today?

"Friday Mood: Fit & Fab Friday - Being Fit and Fab starts with your mind; stop that stinking thinking and unpack those issues that are deep in your tissues...let's get our minds right so we can get our grinds right! I declare and decree that you are Fit, Fabulous and you are walking in God's favor." – Towandaism

Envision IT!

Manifest IT!

ACTIVATE IT!

What's going to be your "go-to" word today?

"Love does; It's not intentions, it's not trying to do. Love does." – Towandaism

Envision IT!

Manifest IT!

ACTIVATE IT!

What's going to be your "go-to" word today?

"I don't know who this message is for; Don't give up, don't give in, hold on, you can make it! Hang on, don't you want to see how you will WIN in the end? Give it one more try, one more prayer, one more push! You are stronger than your trials and tribulations." – Towandaism

Envision IT!

Manifest IT!

ACTIVATE IT!

What's going to be your "go-to" word today?

"Just like Jacob wrestled with the archangel until he blessed him; I need you to wrestle with life and the universe until it delivers ALL that has been earmarked for you! Don't dare give up! Yes, you might walk away with a limp like Jacob, but I promise you it will be worth it! Besides it is better to walk through life with a limp and blessed immeasurably, than to be whole in body and poor in mind, spirit, soul, finances, blessings, possibilities, purpose and passion." – Towandaism

Envision IT!

Manifest IT!

ACTIVATE IT!

What's going to be your "go-to" word today?

"Begin with Prayers, grind, hustle, grind, hustle, grind, End with Prayers!" – Towandaism

Envision IT!

Manifest IT!

ACTIVATE IT!

What's going to be your "go-to" word today?

"It's let Freedom Flow Day! It's time to let go whatever has been weighing you down, forgive all those who have done you wrong, let go all the trials and tribulations of this week, and most importantly it's time to **FORGIVE** yourself for all the things you did not get right up to this point in your life, business, family etc...let freedom flow this **DAY!**" – Towandaism

Envision IT!

Manifest IT!

ACTIVATE IT!

What's going to be your "go-to" word today?

"GET IT DONE NOW! 'Tomorrow must be the longest day of the week – judging from the number of things we will do then!' We push many a thing to 'tomorrow' when, in fact, the Bible tells us that 'you don't know the first thing about tomorrow' (James 4:14 The Message). MAKE IT HAPPEN TODAY!"
– Towandaism

Envision IT!

Manifest IT!

ACTIVATE IT!

What's going to be your "go-to" word today?

"So many of us are crushing under the weight of life, and some days are heavier than others—let's lighten the load by surrendering whatever trial, tribulation or test we are going through to God, right NOW! So, complete this statement, "I surrender_____!" – Towandaism

Envision IT!

Manifest IT!

ACTIVATE IT!

What's going to be your "go-to" word today?

"Today's the day you make it into the "Two Comma Club, naw, let's say SEVEN Comma Club" seek it, speak it, achieve it (manifest it)!" – Towandaism

Envision IT!

Manifest IT!

ACTIVATE IT!

What's going to be your "go-to" word today?

"Woman, cannot live and be successful by GRIND alone." – Towandaism

Envision IT!

Manifest IT!

ACTIVATE IT!

What's going to be your "go-to" word today?

"Money doesn't make me happy; Happiness and joy are choices. However, wise wealth provides access, possibilities and freedom. It's unconditional financial freedom that unshackles me from a nine to five mindset, limitations and traditional norms that excites me." – Towandaism

Envision IT!

Manifest IT!

ACTIVATE IT!

What's going to be your "go-to" word today?

"IT's Fearless Freedom Friday! Walk in your freedom today and Fearlessly Love, Serve, Act, Dream or unapologetically Do You! I see success, prosperity, good health, immeasurable love and earthshaking joy in your very near Future!" – Towandaism

Envision IT!

Manifest IT!

ACTIVATE IT!

What's going to be your "go-to" word today?

I ABORT...

"Abort ALL lying Seeds! You will not take root here...move on!

Abort I am not good enough!

Abort I am not healed!

Abort I am not qualified!

Abort I am a failure!

Abort I am a victim!

Abort I am not wealthy!

Abort I am not prosperous!

Abort I am not successful!

Abort I am not excellent!

Abort I am not highly competent!

Abort I am not capable!

Abort all that is impossible!

Abort I am not a woman of purpose!

Abort I am not thriving!

Abort I am controlled by mental bondage!

Abort I am not built for this time, reason and season!

Abort I am pitiful, miserable and a source of negativity!

Abort that I am not blessed!

Abort shame!

Abort I am a mess and messy!

Abort self-sabotage!

Abort I am not intelligent!

Abort self-loathing!

Abort I can't make it!

Abort stress!

Abort depression!

Abort I deserve less than the best!

Abort I am not talented!

Abort I am not creative!

Abort I have a chip on my shoulder!

Abort stinking thinking!

Abort I am a member of the "toos" I am too loud, too fat, too dark, too tall, too short, too poor, too confident, too aggressive, too proud, too ambitious, too kind, too generous, too loving, too strong, too competent, and too capable!

Abort I am not a daughter of the GREATEST King!

Abort I came from nothing and will never be nothing!

Abort I am not a woman of possibilities!

Abort I will always be Eve and never be a Mary, Ruth or Esther!

So, trolls stroll on, devil you must level up, haters skate your hateful asses on! I am her; the one God has anointed and appointed for greatness, and a tsunami of blessings; and I am claiming all he has ordained for me!"

What do you **ABORT?** This means that you have called it out of its hiding place and dispelled it from your conscious and subconscious self. It cannot hide any longer, you have shined divine light on it and we bury it **TODAY!** Say it out loud, write in your journal, make a video diary of all that you **ABORT** from your life today. Refer to your list as often as needed to remind yourself that you are lightening the load you have been carrying. Where you are headed this baggage will not serve you. So, whether it is a person, place, thing, or a poisoned seed someone has planted in you, today you are aborting it today. Repeat after me, "I **ABORT**...!" Keep going until you have exhausted all the baggage you have been carrying, because we are leaving it all in baggage claim with no luggage tag so it will not return to you. You are soaring now! Drop that **LOAD** of garage and mark it return-to-sender!" – Towandaism

Envision IT!

Manifest IT!

ACTIVATE IT!

What's going to be your "go-to" word today?

Grace-
Divine Advantage

"Stand back, those cracks you are seeing in my armor is my greatness breaking through!"—Towandaism

Envision IT!

Manifest IT!

ACTIVATE IT!

What's going to be your "go-to" word today?

"A LIFE interrupted by GOD, is a LIFE put back on course to fulfill God's assignment and achieve successes beyond human measure." — Towandaism

Envision IT!

Manifest IT!

ACTIVATE IT!

What's going to be your "go-to" word today?

"Sometimes you just have to let Silence sit and stay for a while, because it is in those moments of silence you develop your most powerful authentic voice." – Towandaism

Envision IT!

Manifest IT!

ACTIVATE IT!

What's going to be your "go-to" word today?

"Avoiding healing is not going to change what has happened to you in the past, however it will prevent you from showing up great now and in the future." – Towandaism

Envision IT!

Manifest IT!

ACTIVATE IT!

What's going to be your "go-to" word today?

"Self-awareness is the mirror that escapes me; God, reveal your me." – Towandaism

Envision IT!

Manifest IT!

ACTIVATE IT!

What's going to be your "go-to" word today?

"The mess is yours, however the message is authored by God." – Towandaism

Envision IT!

Manifest IT!

ACTIVATE IT!

What's going to be your "go-to" word today?

"You can only hide your STUFF for so long before you break, so get therapy and seek Jesus!"
– Towandaism

Envision IT!

Manifest IT!

ACTIVATE IT!

What's going to be your "go-to" word today?

"Sometimes all you can give is grace, and sometimes all you need is grace. Generously, dispense grace, and grace will be poured on you, poured for you and drawn to you." – Towandaism

Envision IT!

Manifest IT!

ACTIVATE IT!

What's going to be your "go-to" word today?

"Those lies they have been saying about you and those lies you keep telling yourself—THEY have an expiration date and TODAY is that day!" – Towandaism

Envision IT!

Manifest IT!

ACTIVATE IT!

What's going to be your "go-to" word today?

"Knowing him makes it impossible to doubt him. Some days I feel unworthy, but I thank Jesus for knowing I was worth it!" – Towandaism

Envision IT!

Manifest IT!

ACTIVATE IT!

What's going to be your "go-to" word today?

"God, I must get to Heaven, there are some people waiting for me there. So, Holy Spirit, guide my actions, steps and words. Help me, Holy Spirit, arrive halo and wings ready! In Jesus name, it's so by faith and by faith so it is. Amen and Amen!" – Towandaism

Envision IT!

Manifest IT!

ACTIVATE IT!

What's going to be your "go-to" word today?

"If you are struggling and unsure of your next move--Give more and Serve more, you will find yourself there." – Towandaism

Envision IT!

Manifest IT!

ACTIVATE IT!

What's going to be your "go-to" word today?

"So many are living in a Spiritual Desert and they are in need of a Divine Deluge; praying without ceasing is a must." – Towandaism

Envision IT!

Manifest IT!

ACTIVATE IT!

What's going to be your "go-to" word today?

If you're lit, light someone else's candle, you will shine brighter. – Towandaism

Envision IT!

Manifest IT!

ACTIVATE IT!

What's going to be your "go-to" word today?

"There is power in patience, there is power in the process, and there is power in prayer...just hold on!"
– Towandaism

Envision IT!

Manifest IT!

ACTIVATE IT!

What's going to be your "go-to" word today?

"Our children are bombarded with mass distractions, the appeals of affluenza and ugliness of society daily. Therefore, as parents, aunts, uncles and those that fill in the gaps, it is our responsibility to introduce, instruct and lead our children to Jesus. For theirs and future generations salvation, we must show our children the power of God's promises. Is it more important for our children to get into Harvard or Heaven? We must show them that Love Does, Faith Does and Jesus Delivers. We must show them the power of Grace and Forgiveness; and how to use the greatest gifts we have like faith, hope, joy, love and compassion to grow through this human experience." – Towandaism

Envision IT!

Manifest IT!

ACTIVATE IT!

What's going to be your "go-to" word today?

"Some of you are where you are today because your Grandmas, Grandpas, Mothers and Fathers prayed for you; they understood the power of prayer. Now it's your turn to pray for you and yours, because your time is now; and, God has no grandchildren." – Towandaism

Envision IT!

Manifest IT!

ACTIVATE IT!

What's going to be your "go-to" word today?

"We have become a world that rather accepts 'the lying truth' than the truthful facts. We rather co-sign to comfortable lies, than fight for freedoms, fairness, facts, and our faith." – Towandaism

Envision IT!

Manifest IT!

ACTIVATE IT!

What's going to be your "go-to" word today?

"Man will give you awards; however, God dispenses rewards!" – Towandaism

Envision IT!

Manifest IT!

ACTIVATE IT!

What's going to be your "go-to" word today?

"God can write straight on a crooked line; he has prepared your path; he is with you on your journey; and your name is being spoken and praised in rooms and spaces you have yet to enter." – Towandaism

Envision IT!

Manifest IT!

ACTIVATE IT!

What's going to be your "go-to" word today?

"Stop poisoning your earmarked promises, prosperity and endless possibilities with your problems, ill-circumstances or bitterness! Trust that God is in it, and you will Win it!" – Towandaism

Envision IT!

Manifest IT!

ACTIVATE IT!

What's going to be your "go-to" word today?

"More change has occurred in the world through prayer than voting; so, while you are voting remain in constant prayer." – Towandaism

Envision IT!

Manifest IT!

ACTIVATE IT!

What's going to be your "go-to" word today?

"Mental health maintenance is a **MUST** if you truly want to live your best life and be a person of value and is valued. Being truly wealthy means having a healthy mind, body, soul, spirit and, oh yeah, bank account."

– Towandaism

Envision IT!

Manifest IT!

ACTIVATE IT!

What's going to be your "go-to" word today?

"Don't confuse looking great with being great; an apple can look red and delicious on the outside and rotten to the core on the inside." – Towandaism

Envision IT!

Manifest IT!

ACTIVATE IT!

What's going to be your "go-to" word today?

"Imagine what would happen if you stop blaming and start becoming!" – Towandaism

Envision IT!

Manifest IT!

ACTIVATE IT!

What's going to be your "go-to" word today?

"Every day you need to unplug from the world so you can hear God speak, listen to his message, receive his word and more importantly obey his guidance." – Towandaism

Envision IT!

Manifest IT!

ACTIVATE IT!

What's going to be your "go-to" word today?

"You may be facing financial challenges at home or in businesses; or you may be experiencing lack in some area of your life. I want you to know, like Gideon and David (in the Bible), we too must learn not to depend on numbers, but to depend on God. Your immeasurable blessings are here!" – Towandaism

Envision IT!

Manifest IT!

ACTIVATE IT!

What's going to be your "go-to" word today?

"Sister to Sister or Sister to Brother!!! Practice Self-Care, which is Self-Love! Please make a habit of managing your health needs, which includes your mind, body, soul and spirit. Go for your check-ups and check-ins! Go to the doctors, dentist, therapist, financial adviser and most importantly, take it all to God, the Master Healer and Provider.

I know you are grinding, I know you are making it happen, I know you have bills to pay, debt to reduce, children & ailing parents to care for etc...; all of this will not matter if you become seriously ill, or worse, you die from a preventable disease or issue. So, not only get your mind right to get your grind right; get your body and health right, get your finances right, get your spirit right!

Look Fam! We need you on this side of heaven, so, please take excellent care of yourself. Your indelible impact and bright light continues to touch many! Your presence on this earth is impacting folks you haven't met yet and may never meet. May God's Kingdom Favor chase you down daily and shower with immeasurable blessings. Be well and Live well!" – Towandaism

Envision IT!

Manifest IT!

ACTIVATE IT!

What's going to be your "go-to" word today?

"Don't let the saturation of social ills' news clips on social media make you doubt him, because you know too much about him, **GOD IS WINNING,** the salvation will be televised!" – Towandaism

Envision IT!

Manifest IT!

ACTIVATE IT!

What's going to be your "go-to" word today?

"More and more people are turning to governments to fix societal ills, instead of turning to GOD. If you think more man-made laws, rules and regulations are going to change the corrupt conditions, moral decay and apathy in our world; you are wrong! More prayer, more love, more serving and more giving, more compassion, more God--that is what is going to change our world; the breaking of generational curses and transforming our minds will save ALL nations." – Towandaism

Envision IT!

Manifest IT!

ACTIVATE IT!

What's going to be your "go-to" word today?

"You must respect my rise! Out of the ashes of life, out of the hate and negativity, out of failures and messy mistakes, out of the guilt and shame, and out of loss and grief; You MUST respect my rise!" – Towandaism

Envision IT!

Manifest IT!

ACTIVATE IT!

What's going to be your "go-to" word today?

"Wisdom, like entrepreneurship, is what you seek; however, it is a process that many cannot endure. Be patient, endure the process and your prosperity and wisdom will be immeasurable." – Towandaism

Envision IT!

Manifest IT!

ACTIVATE IT!

What's going to be your "go-to" word today?

"Why must the growing catalysts for sustainable equality and freedom that benefits every generation, nation or people be fertilized by the blood of Black folks and the tears of Black Mothers and Fathers?"

– Towandaism

Envision IT!

Manifest IT!

ACTIVATE IT!

What's going to be your "go-to" word today?

"Imagine how mad the devil is going to be when you reach your divine destination, when you prosper, when you succeed, when you excel in spite of all the crap, minions, hate, evil and obstacles he throws at you...let's make his miserable ass MAD! Arise Champion! Win Warrior!" – Towandaism

Envision IT!

Manifest IT!

ACTIVATE IT!

What's going to be your "go-to" word today?

"Given all that has happened, is happening and will happen, I know prayer is the response and God is the answer. Also, I know faith, hope, love and dreams without action are worthless." – Towandaism

Envision IT!

Manifest IT!

ACTIVATE IT!

What's going to be your "go-to" word today?

"Finding yourself in the dark, having issues, and needing help? Get at me!" – God (-Towandaism)

Envision IT!

Manifest IT!

ACTIVATE IT!

What's going to be your "go-to" word today?

"Give more, serve more - you will find yourself there." – Towandaism

Envision IT!

Manifest IT!

ACTIVATE IT!

What's going to be your "go-to" word today?

"I'm Praying without ceasing-Wow, The Power of Prayer-Prayer moves people and things into positions to elevate you and block those things or people who mean you harm." – Towandaism

Envision IT!

Manifest IT!

ACTIVATE IT!

What's going to be your "go-to" word today?

"I get extremely disappointed when folks find themselves in challenging situations that violate the moral fabric of humanity and 'take a pass' on doing something about it, speaking out against it, or stand up for those who can't stand up for themselves, in the moment; and those who acquiesce to flawed laws. They state, 'It's not my job or responsibility,'; well, YES, it is theirs and our job and responsibility. Freedom, equity, equality, peace and the wellbeing of ALL is our responsibility. True character is revealed under pressure!" – Towandaism

Envision IT!

Manifest IT!

ACTIVATE IT!

What's going to be your "go-to" word today?

"Black men can now officially be added to the endangered species; will they now get more resources, opportunities and protection so they can thrive? Will we now respect their lives as much as everyone else's? We have to do more than publish reports and be spectators to this modern day erasing of our sons, brothers, fathers, uncles and husbands..." – Towandaism

Envision IT!

Manifest IT!

ACTIVATE IT!

What's going to be your "go-to" word today?

"There's something about the name JESUS! When things are going left; all you need to do is Shout JESUS, and he steps in! Suddenly, there is a course correction! AMEN!" – Towandaism

Envision IT!

Manifest IT!

ACTIVATE IT!

What's going to be your "go-to" word today?

"Stake your claim today! Whether it is good health, great wealth, peace of mind, a new career, the love of your life...whatever IT is, stake your claim!" – Towandaism

Envision IT!

Manifest IT!

ACTIVATE IT!

What's going to be your "go-to" word today?

"A Butterfly can never go back to being a caterpillar, however a caterpillar can become a Butterfly. A Butterfly can mentally still be a caterpillar, but her new wings will not let her go back to old things. She must accept, adjust and fly." – Towandaism

Envision IT!

Manifest IT!

ACTIVATE IT!

What's going to be your "go-to" word today?

"I hate to spoil the ending for you, but Jesus wins!" – Towandaism

Envision IT!

Manifest IT!

ACTIVATE IT!

What's going to be your "go-to" word today?

"May today be the day you awaken from that permanent nod State you have been so comfortable living in, so that your life can be flooded with Untrammeled Success, prosperity, love and purpose." – Towandaism

Envision IT!

Manifest IT!

ACTIVATE IT!

What's going to be your "go-to" word today?

"Patience my friend your blessings are about to blow your mind...you are not planting flowers expecting bulbs, you are planting bulbs in expectation of an abundance of beautiful flowers...patience, IT is already yours!" – Towandaism

Envision IT!

Manifest IT!

ACTIVATE IT!

What's going to be your "go-to" word today?

"May the God in me be greater than the devil in me today." – Towandaism

Envision IT!

Manifest IT!

ACTIVATE IT!

What's going to be your "go-to" word today?

"Be a laser light not a flood light. GET FOCUS!" – Towandaism

Envision IT!

Manifest IT!

ACTIVATE IT!

What's going to be your "go-to" word today?

"God, find me where you know I need to be." – Towandaism

Envision IT!

Manifest IT!

ACTIVATE IT!

What's going to be your "go-to" word today?

"I'm Feeding my dreams and starving my fears! Although the journey, the becoming and the growing is tough, painful and scary; I'm tougher, purpose-driven, and courageous; because, I was born and built for a time such as this. I'm pressing on and praying upwards. To God be the Glory!" – Towandaism

Envision IT!

Manifest IT!

ACTIVATE IT!

What's going to be your "go-to" word today?

"He will turn your "mess-to-pieces" to masterpieces...ask and you will receive, seek and you will find and knock and all will be open to you." – Towandaism

Envision IT!

Manifest IT!

ACTIVATE IT!

What's going to be your "go-to" word today?

"I know a lot of people and things are pulling, pulling and pulling on you, your spirit...know that whatever is pulling on you is not greater or more powerful than what and who is **PUSHING YOU!** Your purpose and passion are **PUSHING YOU!** Your Faith and God are **PUSHING YOU!**" – Towandaism

Envision IT!

Manifest IT!

ACTIVATE IT!

What's going to be your "go-to" word today?

"There are only a few Prisoners of War (POWs) I've taken that no one can rescue: My Faith in God, Success, Excellence, Love, Hope, Passion, My Purpose and Possibilities. Come and try to save them, I dare you!" – Towandaism

Envision IT!

Manifest IT!

ACTIVATE IT!

What's going to be your "go-to" word today?

"We often get drunk on money, power, position, people, and love for things; TIME'S UP! It is TIME to SOBER UP, with laser-like focus tap into your God-given greatness and deliver on your assignment! Someone is struggling because you are playing it safe, they need you to do your part, so they can live up their greatness. You have to decide right now to either be a spectator or a player in this life; do you really want to witness someone else enjoying a blessing that was earmarked for you? Sober Up!" – Towandaism

Envision IT!

Manifest IT!

ACTIVATE IT!

What's going to be your "go-to" word today?

"There is a fire that is inside of me that burns like a tsunami of infernos; it is bright as a trillion suns; it is all consuming. It incinerates all fears and doubts; it illuminates hope, faith, love. It turns the ashes of my failures to the nourishment for my successes. It chokes out mediocrities and bolsters my will, insatiable drive for divine excellence. It chars my weaknesses and multiplies my strengths. It dries my tears leaving behind the salt of life. This fire was ignited by God and no man or worldly possessions can extinguish it; I have to feed the flame by strutting in my God-given purpose...it is hungry for my greatness, successes and excellence; and this hunger fuels my courage to pursue the divine options of servitude, generosity, forgiveness and gratitude. I feel the burn; do you see the light?"

– Towanda's song (Towandaism 2018)

Envision IT!

Manifest IT!

ACTIVATE IT!

What's going to be your "go-to" word today?

"I do not have the mental capacity to understand the power, compassion, love, grace and mercy of God...sorry, Lord for the limitations of my mind and THANK YOU Lord for your immeasurable blessings and love." – Towandaism

Envision IT!

Manifest IT!

ACTIVATE IT!

What's going to be your "go-to" word today?

"How can I not rise while riding on the wings of God's most-fiercest Guardian Angels—see no man can stop what God has ordained." – Towandaism

Envision IT!

Manifest IT!

ACTIVATE IT!

What's going to be your "go-to" word today?

"Everybody wants to go heaven, but no one wants to die; everybody wants the glory, but no one wants to live through the story; everybody wants the sunshine, but will not walk in the rain; everybody wants to win, but no one wants to endure a loss; and everybody wants to be a butterfly, but no one wants to be a caterpillar." – Towandaism

Envision IT!

Manifest IT!

ACTIVATE IT!

What's going to be your "go-to" word today?

"In life as in business, be careful, you never know who is watching, and it is getting harder and harder to distinguish your biggest fans from your worst enemies." – Towandaism

Envision IT!

Manifest IT!

ACTIVATE IT!

What's going to be your "go-to" word today?

"May the peace of God and his perfect Holy Spirit surround and fill you, overflow around you, in you, through you and to you abundantly and generously. This perfect and divine peace goes with you as a pillar of cloud by day and a pillar of fire by night. Thank you, Lord!" – Towandaism

Envision IT!

Manifest IT!

ACTIVATE IT!

What's going to be your "go-to" word today?

"Stop looking for the answer; the answer to your successes is YOU; the answer to your failures is YOU...the reason why you exist is because you are the answer to someone's questions and prayers! So, what the hell are you waiting for, get on your grind!" – Towandaism

Envision IT!

Manifest IT!

ACTIVATE IT!

What's going to be your "go-to" word today?

"The doors will open for those who have the courage to kick the motherfuckers in!" – Towandaism

Envision IT!

Manifest IT!

ACTIVATE IT!

What's going to be your "go-to" word today?

"We live forward and learn backwards. Use your wisdom to elevate, empower and enable others; and your greatness will shine!" – Towandaism

Envision IT!

Manifest IT!

ACTIVATE IT!

What's going to be your "go-to" word today?

"Enough IS Enough!!! Enough with the hate; Enough with the violence; Enough with the shootings; Enough with senseless crimes and murder of Black and Brown people; Enough with the sexual harassment; Enough with the plagues of drugs and addictions; Enough with not finding our missing; Enough with poor leadership; Enough with Fake News; Enough with cops killing us; Enough with us killing us; Enough with Flint not having clean water; Enough with homelessness in America; Enough with building walls; Enough with killing our babies; Enough with pedophiles; Enough with domestic violence; Enough with bullying; Enough with mass distractions; Enough with intentional ignorance; Enough with hunger; Enough with human trafficking; Enough with phony politicians; Enough with greed; Enough with self-hate; Enough with lack of health and wellness programs; Enough with teachers and schools not having much needed skills and supplies; Enough with one-percenters; Enough with the gun violence; Enough with the lack of empathy, compassion and love; Enough with all the talk; Enough with not addressing mental illness; Enough with not sharing the CURE; Enough with Threats of Nuclear War; Enough with threats of chemical warfare; Enough with North Korea and Russia; Enough with unemployment...what are your 'Enough with' statements?" – Towandaism

Envision IT!

Manifest IT!

ACTIVATE IT!

What's going to be your "go-to" word today?

"What if the total destruction or inferno that has turned your life/world/business upside down (it may be a personal or professional crisis); was God's way of letting you know that you have outgrown these circumstances and pushing you to greatness, immeasurable success, and extraordinary excellence?"

– Towandaism

Envision IT!

Manifest IT!

ACTIVATE IT!

What's going to be your "go-to" word today?

"I was wondering if God prays, and if so, who does he pray to and for?" – Towandaism

Envision IT!

Manifest IT!

ACTIVATE IT!

What's going to be your "go-to" word today?

"From the lost to the cross you paid the cost; thank you Lord Jesus our Savior!" – Towandaism

Envision IT!

Manifest IT!

ACTIVATE IT!

What's going to be your "go-to" word today?

"Have you received gifts that you have never opened? I'm going to presume you have not. So, why haven't you opened God's gifts to you? What are you waiting for? Tear into your God-given gifts and watch your life of abundance flow!" – Towandaism

Envision IT!

Manifest IT!

ACTIVATE IT!

What's going to be your "go-to" word today?

"Invest In the mental/physical well-being of your team, employees and partners, because they are your most valuable asset, because absenteeism and presenteeism come with costly price tag that erodes the value you generate for your customers, the value you manifest through your team, your profits, and most importantly the quality of life of your team." – Towandaism

Envision IT!

Manifest IT!

ACTIVATE IT!

What's going to be your "go-to" word today?

"The illumination of your path requires sight beyond sight, wisdom beyond wisdom and a keen ear for that God Inspired voice." – Towandaism

Envision IT!

Manifest IT!

ACTIVATE IT!

What's going to be your "go-to" word today?

"Every obstacle you faced up to this point was to help you build your emotional muscle, stop crying why me, say with confidence TRY ME!" – Towandaism

Envision IT!

Manifest IT!

ACTIVATE IT!

What's going to be your "go-to" word today?

"I'm committed as a servant leader to not just take your business/career to the next level, but to a new **REALM,** a new stratosphere!" – Towandaism

Envision IT!

Manifest IT!

ACTIVATE IT!

What's going to be your "go-to" word today?

"Sins always lead to slavery of one kind or another." – Towandaism

Envision IT!

Manifest IT!

ACTIVATE IT!

What's going to be your "go-to" word today?

"The God in you will not let you fail, break, or give up!" – Towandaism

Envision IT!

Manifest IT!

ACTIVATE IT!

What's going to be your "go-to" word today?

"Forgive me for not paying attention to your messiness, child, I was focused on my Goals!" – Towandaism

Envision IT!

Manifest IT!

ACTIVATE IT!

What's going to be your "go-to" word today?

"The most disrespectful action that you are doing to yourself is ignoring your Purpose and Passion. So, get to it!" – Towandaism

Envision IT!

Manifest IT!

ACTIVATE IT!

What's going to be your "go-to" word today?

"Do not limit God's supernatural plans for you —you are a masterpiece!" – Towandaism

Envision IT!

Manifest IT!

ACTIVATE IT!

What's going to be your "go-to" word today?

"C.R.O.W.N stands for:

Courageous

Resilient

Optimistic

Wise

Nurturer

Crowns Up! Wear yours well!" – Towandaism

Envision IT!

Manifest IT!

ACTIVATE IT!

What's going to be your "go-to" word today?

"Wear winning like an attitude. Make winning your habit. Make winning your lifestyle. If you must wear a label, make it WINNER!" – Towandaism

Envision IT!

Manifest IT!

ACTIVATE IT!

What's going to be your "go-to" word today?

"They say the most important meal of the day is breakfast. I agree. My breakfast is the word of God, so, I devour his word to command my day and nourish my soul." – Towandaism

Envision IT!

Manifest IT!

ACTIVATE IT!

What's going to be your "go-to" word today?

"Bitter or Better, the choice is yours; choose carefully your success and prosperity hinges on your decision!" – Towandaism

Envision IT!

Manifest IT!

ACTIVATE IT!

What's going to be your "go-to" word today?

"Do not pay attention to social media, the news or the negativity—God is winning!"
– Towandaism

Envision IT!

Manifest IT!

ACTIVATE IT!

What's going to be your "go-to" word today?

"Fake news is a mass distraction that is being used to divide us, deceive us, discourage us and damage us. Before you share, care!" – Towandaism

Envision IT!

Manifest IT!

ACTIVATE IT!

What's going to be your "go-to" word today?

"I breathe in fire and exhale infernos of hope, compassion, prosperity and love. Stand in my path and you will be consumed by these wildfires and reborn a flame." – Towandaism

Envision IT!

Manifest IT!

ACTIVATE IT!

What's going to be your "go-to" word today?

"Some of you are worried about how many followers you have; and God is saying, 'I thought you were my follower! I thought you were following my divine post, following my divine news feed, and tuning into my divine tweets! Put down that phone and pick up your Bible, all the answers you seek are in your hands; and the influence and prosperity you seek is at the tip of your tongue. Every time I call you to have a dialogue, I go straight to voicemail. My child, I'm here waiting on you, you will never have to wait for me. I am in you, with you at ALL times. I am not bound by time, but you are my child...let's talk soon.' " – Towandaism

Envision IT!

Manifest IT!

ACTIVATE IT!

What's going to be your "go-to" word today?

"Dear Friend, I have a gift for you today, here it is, this Key! This Key is going to set you free and unleash your awesomeness, your greatness and your possibilities. Here, my friend, is the Key, use this key to forgive yourself, it does not matter the deed, today you are free with this key. Here, my friend, is the Key, use this Key to unshackle yourself from toxic people; see they are weighing your wings down and it is your time to fly, no soar, into your greatness. Here you go my friend, use this Key to save yourself from the "negative self-talk" bondage that has you repeating self-destructive behaviors. My friend, please accept this Key to rescue you from distractions, discouragement and deception, so, with laser-like focus the path to your winning season will forever be illuminated. Take this Key release all of those pent-up tears and emotions, let them go, it's okay if the tears flow, the tears must flow because it's time to cleanse your mind, heart and soul, so, you can shift into gear to claim the best version of You. Please, my friend, accept my gift, accept this Key, the world needs your gifts, talents, and greatness. One last Key for you my friend, please use this Key to bind, lock away or cast out forever ALL the diabolical people and plans that have undermined your greatness and have tried to dull your Shine. You are now FREE my friend, relish this freedom and use this freedom to claim and own your God-given purpose, passion and limitless prosperity. You are more than WORTHY, my friend."

– Warmest regards, Your Friend, Towandaism

Envision IT!

Manifest IT!

ACTIVATE IT!

What's going to be your "go-to" word today?

"Are you a ladder climber or a ladder builder? I can honestly state early in my career my ambition blinded me and I was a ladder climber, until I realized that I could empower and enable many by being a ladder builder. Ensuring others success and serving others have blessed me beyond measure." – Towandaism

Envision IT!

Manifest IT!

ACTIVATE IT!

What's going to be your "go-to" word today?

"As temperatures rise so do tempers, please be more kind, patient, loving and compassionate. Life is too short; cherish every moment and remember you are worthy of an abundant life." – Towandaism

Envision IT!

Manifest IT!

ACTIVATE IT!

What's going to be your "go-to" word today?

"GPS is the acronym for God's Prayer System, activate it!" – Towandaism

Envision IT!

Manifest IT!

ACTIVATE IT!

What's going to be your "go-to" word today?

"Ask and you will receive, seek and you will find and knock and all will be open to you...yes, I have faith."

– Towandaism

Envision IT!

Manifest IT!

ACTIVATE IT!

What's going to be your "go-to" word today?

"God has given me wisdom beyond wisdom, sight beyond sight and divine hearing, listening and learning...God has made me a successful strategist." – Towandaism

Envision IT!

Manifest IT!

ACTIVATE IT!

What's going to be your "go-to" word today?

"My redemption is in my divine risk-taking." — Towandaism

Envision IT!

Manifest IT!

ACTIVATE IT!

What's going to be your "go-to" word today?

"I'm fearlessly Faithful in God and the God in me, and I receive all my spiritual strategies.

My Next is my divine leveling up!" – Towandaism

Envision IT!

Manifest IT!

ACTIVATE IT!

What's going to be your "go-to" word today?

"More give more; more serves more; more do more; more achieve more; more invest more; more educate more; more enrich more; more empower more; more help more; and more thank more! What's your MORE?" – Towandaism

Envision IT!

Manifest IT!

ACTIVATE IT!

What's going to be your "go-to" word today?

"When your faith in YOU waivers, borrow God's faith in YOU! You are purposefully Possible and wonderfully Worthy!" – Towandaism

Envision IT!

Manifest IT!

ACTIVATE IT!

What's going to be your "go-to" word today?

"Know that if your flame starts to flicker or dim, your Posse will be there to lend you their flames; see, you were never meant to be a basic bonfire, you were always an eternal inferno of possibilities and prosperity."
– Towandaism

Envision IT!

Manifest IT!

ACTIVATE IT!

What's going to be your "go-to" word today?

"Your journey in life is your story to tell, so make it epic and remember all those mistakes and failures you made along the way are plot twists and will make your legacy legendary...no one likes a boring story."
– Towandaism

Envision IT!

Manifest IT!

ACTIVATE IT!

What's going to be your "go-to" word today?

"Speak Up Sunday - speak life, love and enlightenment into your dreams and goals. Put a demand on Heaven and the Universe to release all that has been promised to you, that's in your favor and all the supernatural strength to slay ALL Goliaths in your path. Claim your True Place today!" – Towandaism

Envision IT!

Manifest IT!

ACTIVATE IT!

What's going to be your "go-to" word today?

"Dream Big, Bodacious, Behemoth Dreams; Dream with BOLDNESS and take the limits off of God!"
– Towandaism

Envision IT!

Manifest IT!

ACTIVATE IT!

What's going to be your "go-to" word today?

"You know I weep inside every time I hear a girl or woman say I can't, it's impossible or I won't make it succeed. The lies we tell ourselves only serve to keep us from greatness..." – Towandaism

Envision IT!

Manifest IT!

ACTIVATE IT!

What's going to be your "go-to" word today?

"Yep, I'm a practicing and participating Disciple. I'm a disciple of God's Grace, entrepreneurship, excellence, success, prosperity, abundance, servitude, compassion, faith, love...discipleship, only the strong need apply!" – Towandaism

Envision IT!

Manifest IT!

ACTIVATE IT!

What's going to be your "go-to" word today?

"Yes, it's the thrill of divine possibilities that forces me to make space, make room, and move stuff out of the way, so, that ALL women (and girls) can see, feel and believe their dreams are possible too. It's the one thing that is buried deep in me that compels me to keep moving, keep looking up, keep getting up no matter the storm, tsunami, tornado, hurricane I face; and it's this one thing I pray I awaken in all girls and women...that one thing is HOPE!" – Towandaism

Envision IT!

Manifest IT!

ACTIVATE IT!

What's going to be your "go-to" word today?

"Broken women, raise broken children, fall in love and even marry broken men, surround themselves with broken friends —all to feed their broken spirit. Enter God! God uses the very things that broke her as a catalyst to elevate her, heal her, transform her, and strengthen her. Generational curses are broken, her children are thriving, she has attracted genuine love and she now keeps company with friends who uplift her. Never underestimate a broken woman cloaked in God's Grace and Favor." – Towandaism

Envision IT!

Manifest IT!

ACTIVATE IT!

What's going to be your "go-to" word today?

There is a point in your life that your relationships with your girlfriends transcend friendship and give birth to sisters and an unbreakable, unshakable and unyielding sisterhood! My sisters, Rhonda, Molina and LaShawn showed up and showed out; they loved up on me and words cannot begin to express the overflow of love I'm feeling; This is my **PRAISE REPORT!** Some folks are lucky to have one bestie in life, I have been blessed with Ten!" – Towandaism

Envision IT!

Manifest IT!

ACTIVATE IT!

What's going to be your "go-to" word today?

"You thought I was falling apart, umm actually I was falling into place with grace." –
Towandaism

Envision IT!

Manifest IT!

ACTIVATE IT!

What's going to be your "go-to" word today?

"Life and death are at the tip of your tongue; the **POWER** of the **WORD** (spoken or mere thoughts) can speak life, light and enlightenment into your dreams, goals, good health, great wealth, success, freedom (from debt bondage, self-hate, self-sabotage, abuse, addiction, bad habits or carnal proclivities), business, career, and your next level. The power of the word can kill them all too! Guard your mouth, your words, and your thoughts." – Towandaism

Envision IT!

Manifest IT!

ACTIVATE IT!

What's going to be your "go-to" word today?

"STOP comparing your life to the highlight reels of others' lives on social media! Live, move and talk with purpose on purpose! Folks' glory moments are not the stories that they had to live through to get where they are. It doesn't matter what you are going through at this very moment, you are about to give the devil two black eyes!" – Towandaism

Envision IT!

Manifest IT!

ACTIVATE IT!

What's going to be your "go-to" word today?

"PURPOSE is poison to failure!" – Towandaism

Envision IT!

Manifest IT!

ACTIVATE IT!

What's going to be your "go-to" word today?

"Pain and suffering do not discriminate; however, neither does blessings and healing." – Towandaism

Envision IT!

Manifest IT!

ACTIVATE IT!

What's going to be your "go-to" word today?

"Before you make big (or small) decisions in your life, career, business, or relationships; ask yourself, 'Where's God in this?' Be still and wait for God's response...don't be surprised about the outcome, be blessed and trust God will go before you and pave the way." – Towandaism

Envision IT!

Manifest IT!

ACTIVATE IT!

What's going to be your "go-to" word today?

"You are in a season of becoming; surrender to it with grit, grind and grace; the pruning may be painful, however what's on the other side of the process is worth it."
– Towandaism

Envision IT!

Manifest IT!

ACTIVATE IT!

What's going to be your "go-to" word today?

"Intentionally Win...win on **PURPOSE!**" – Towandaism

Envision IT!

Manifest IT!

ACTIVATE IT!

What's going to be your "go-to" word today?

Towanda R. Livingston

"It is time we realize we are ALL in this TOGETHER and when we hate others, we hate ourselves, when we hurt each other, we hurt ourselves; and when we kill, we kill our chances to rise above the rhetoric and we marginalize humanity...prayers for the Pittsburgh victims and their families; ENOUGH IS ENOUGH! Hate will not WIN!"
– Towandaism

Envision IT!

Manifest IT!

ACTIVATE IT!

What's going to be your "go-to" word today?

390

"We MUST shift from politics to Peopltics; no more politicians but more 'peoplticians'; no more self-interest but much more Our interest; we must take care of our sister, our brother, our neighbor in doing so we ensure our collective peace and prosperity." – Towandaism

Envision IT!

Manifest IT!

ACTIVATE IT!

What's going to be your "go-to" word today?

"Thank you, God, for the doors you closed to protect me and Thank you for answering **NO** to protect me from things I thought I wanted but was not good for me! To God be the Glory, I am still standing! Amen!!!!" – Towandaism

Envision IT!

Manifest IT!

ACTIVATE IT!

What's going to be your "go-to" word today?

"Thank you, God, for working on me, for me and through me ...continue to strengthen me, fix me, change me to break free from limitations and leap into the possibilities of my divine purpose." – Towandaism

Envision IT!

Manifest IT!

ACTIVATE IT!

What's going to be your "go-to" word today?

"The first step is on FAITH; the next step you FLY into your purpose, possibilities and passion!"
– Towandaism

Envision IT!

Manifest IT!

ACTIVATE IT!

What's going to be your "go-to" word today?

"God's delays are not God's denials! Stay tuned in, a tsunami of blessings is about to happen; ready?"

– Towandaism

Envision IT!

Manifest IT!

ACTIVATE IT!

What's going to be your "go-to" word today?

"Everybody is writing but no one is reading, everybody is talking but no one is listening. The answers we are seeking have already been revealed; do more participative reading and more intentional listening."

– Towandaism

Envision IT!

Manifest IT!

ACTIVATE IT!

What's going to be your "go-to" word today?

"Yesterday I received a 'gift' that was hard for me receive and I'm still pondering this 'gift'..."what I know for sure, when I started on my journey on the road towards Excellence there were a few signs posted before I took this road, one read **NO EXIT**, one read **DETOURS AHEAD**, one read **PAY TOLLS AHEAD**, one read **CONSTRUCTION AHEAD**, and the speed limit read, **GOD's SPEED**" — Towandaism!

Envision IT!

Manifest IT!

ACTIVATE IT!

What's going to be your "go-to" word today?

"Relax, Recover, Rejuvenate and then Reign!" – Towandaism

Envision IT!

Manifest IT!

ACTIVATE IT!

What's going to be your "go-to" word today?

"The only thing I will fail in is sin; I'm coming for all God has promised me...I'm claiming all my blessings." – Towandaism

Envision IT!

Manifest IT!

ACTIVATE IT!

What's going to be your "go-to" word today?

"If I trip on the way up the ladder of success, I pray it is because my shoelaces were untied." – Towandaism

Envision IT!

Manifest IT!

ACTIVATE IT!

What's going to be your "go-to" word today?

"In my pursuit for excellence and success, I never wanted to be a Queen, my desire and purpose is to be the Queen-maker and the King-maker...ensuring your success guarantees mine." – Towandaism

Envision IT!

Manifest IT!

ACTIVATE IT!

What's going to be your "go-to" word today?

"You know you are about to experience a breakthrough BLESSING when the enemy sends an army of doubters with discouragement, deception and mass distractions. Stay focus, stay prayed up, and stay the course. You will be the VICTOR and not the VICTIM!" – Towandaism

Envision IT!

Manifest IT!

ACTIVATE IT!

What's going to be your "go-to" word today?

"He saw the dark in me and he still loved me; with just one kiss, the light was let in; now I'm all aglow with not only the love he has for me...with the radiance of the love of me by me." – Towandaism

Envision IT!

Manifest IT!

ACTIVATE IT!

What's going to be your "go-to" word today?

"Life will beat you down, if you let it, it will try to break you at your core, if you let it; I NEED YOU TO SAY, NOT TODAY! Trust me, you have only been bruised not broken, so I need you to arise every day and claim your crown of victory." – Towandaism

Envision IT!

Manifest IT!

ACTIVATE IT!

What's going to be your "go-to" word today?

"I breathe in God's Grace and Mercy and exhale seeds of hope, greatness, prosperity, victory and his favor wherever I go." – Towandaism

Envision IT!

Manifest IT!

ACTIVATE IT!

What's going to be your "go-to" word today?

"Privilege will never trump pain, purpose and possibilities. The color of your skin, your gender, the amount of money in your back account, and how many people of influence you know doesn't matter. You will never escape the pains of life, suffering and death; you will never lessen the possibilities of those with less than you have; and you will **NEVER** defeat a person with **PURPOSE!** The price of privilege is service; until you learn to serve more, give more and do more for others; all of your gains will serve to generationally destroy you." – Towandaism

Envision IT!

Manifest IT!

ACTIVATE IT!

What's going to be your "go-to" word today?

"It is predicted that a million people die every day; if you are reading this message you are among the "blessed to be a live" folks. Death doesn't discriminate! Given this, why are you wasting time, it's time for you to live, love, succeed on PURPOSE! Stop procrastinating and start progressing and producing on PURPOSE!" – Towandaism

Envision IT!

Manifest IT!

ACTIVATE IT!

What's going to be your "go-to" word today?

"At this very moment someone is taking their first breath and someone is taking their last breath; our lives are made up of moments; some of us miss these moments and some of us relish every moment. It is the moments we seize and bask in that add value between our first and last breaths." – Towandaism

Envision IT!

Manifest IT!

ACTIVATE IT!

What's going to be your "go-to" word today?

"It is through my pain I have found my purpose; it is through my suffering I found my true strength, and through downturns in my life I found the courage to conquer and welcome God's unbroken progress for me! In my darkest hour, God was in the mist, I'm grateful!" – Towandaism

Envision IT!

Manifest IT!

ACTIVATE IT!

What's going to be your "go-to" word today?

"There is no substitute for **PRAYER**; there is no Sweeten & Low; no Splenda or no Nutria sweet substitute for the sweetness of being in God's presence and favor; prayer is the divine honey on which all blessings flow." – Towandaism

Envision IT!

Manifest IT!

ACTIVATE IT!

What's going to be your "go-to" word today?

"I have been anointed for this time, reason, and season in my Mother's womb; God has been preparing me for my appointment - I'm not concerned about man shining the light on me; what's important to me is God's light that is shining through me!" – Towandaism

Envision IT!

Manifest IT!

ACTIVATE IT!

What's going to be your "go-to" word today?

"Lord what does my soul need at this moment?" – Towandaism

Envision IT!

Manifest IT!

ACTIVATE IT!

What's going to be your "go-to" word today?

"You were born to be great, so you are a BOA...repeat after me, 'I am Blessed on Arrival' (BOA)."

– Towandaism

Envision IT!

Manifest IT!

ACTIVATE IT!

What's going to be your "go-to" word today?

"I only want one gift from YOU (& for you), yes YOU, and that is to make room for GOD in every aspect of your LIFE!" – Towandaism

Envision IT!

Manifest IT!

ACTIVATE IT!

What's going to be your "go-to" word today?

"Guard your heart and your mind; it's time to clean house mentally, physically and emotionally to make room for the abundance of possibilities, prosperity and peace that has your name on it in 2019 and many years to come!" – Towandaism

Envision IT!

Manifest IT!

ACTIVATE IT!

What's going to be your "go-to" word today?

"May, Mental Health Awareness Month—Wow! I had a visceral response to your blog related to mental health. I grew up around various mental health issues, and in the African American community, we knew something was wrong with Uncle Tommy and Aunt Janine, however it was dismissed or rarely discussed. These family members were locked away in inconspicuous rooms within the home and their outbursts or behaviors were dismissed. There were no doctors, no medications; only prayer. Yep, we tried to pray (without action) their mental health issues away.

The minister and prayer warriors would show up and pray over our family member, with the expectation that they would cast out the devil or break the devil's bond on our family member. I never heard of Mental health professionals or the treatments for mental diseases until I was 15 years old, and my miseducation came not only from my family, neighbors, but also television. Television would show barbaric treatments of folks locked away in mental health facilities, and they were treated with electric shock, lobotomies and other scary methods. Oh, did I state, I was told early on that going crazy, mental disorders, were only reserved for "white folks", yes, mental disorders had white privilege. In my "hood" if you suffered from a mental disorder, you were stigmatized as "being touched," "nutty," "retarded," "crazy," and older women were just going through "the change." As a child, I absorbed my environment and I took my social and cultural cues with me into adulthood and out into the world. You see mental disorders and diseases were the silent killers that lurked, no stalked my hood and family. Folks who suffered were either beaten, locked away in the family homes, or casted out.

I witnessed these people grow up and turn to illicit drugs, homelessness, alcoholism, prostitution, gambling or some other extreme inappropriate behavior to mask this silent monster. I watched as children and women were abused in our community by parents or husbands who suffered from mental disorders. I watched as men who returned from the Vietnam war self-destruct due to lack of proper care. I watched as our self-confidence turned into self-hate because we could not "shake these demons." I watched suicides of family and friends that simply could not cope with their disorders. I could go on, however, I will stop here and strongly encourage that we take action To destigmatize mental disorders and get mental fitness checkups similar to other health exams; I would encourage us to seek treatment for ourselves and our families as soon as the signs appear; I would encourage that we talk openly about these issues and we start or support community-based organizations that have support groups for families that have relatives that are suffering from mental disorders. Oh, have I ever been to a therapist for support, absolutely!!! As an ambitious African American woman seeking excellence, prosperity, love, acceptance and success in a world that denied her access at every turn; a young girl and then woman whose skin was too dark to be beautiful, whose curves were too full, a woman who was born to fail, but built for greatness and fighting every step of the way to achieve it; yeah, I needed non-judgmental support to build my emotional muscle and strengthen my Mentoring Circle, so yep, I, unapologetically, sought out professional therapy starting out at the age of 15 and I have not regretted my decision. For those who are suffering or observing, seek help and support; mental wellness is no longer reserved for "the white folks." – Towanda R. Livingston (May is Mental Health Awareness Month - http://www.mentalhealthamerica.net/may)

Envision IT!

Manifest IT!

ACTIVATE IT!

What's going to be your "go-to" word today?

"Inside every Phenomenal woman are endless phenomenal women!" – Towandaism

Envision IT!

Manifest IT!

ACTIVATE IT!

What's going to be your "go-to" word today?

"Today is the day you are going to resurrect dead dreams, possibilities and purpose; failed marriages/relationships, and dried up opportunities. YES! Today is the day we breathe life back into all that you thought you lost!" – Towandaism

Envision IT!

Manifest IT!

ACTIVATE IT!

What's going to be your "go-to" word today?

"The intentional seeds of wisdom for living a life overflowing with positivity, excellence, greatness, success and abundance that are being planted in me by my circle of influence thus far are priceless, immeasurable and impactful!" – Towandaism

Envision IT!

Manifest IT!

ACTIVATE IT!

What's going to be your "go-to" word today?

"The first year of marriage is tough but not insurmountable. It's hard because you are growing and stretching- you are becoming one - and there will be growing pains - think about it you both have left behind single lives, you came and went as you pleased, you made decisions for yourself, you were responsible for yourself, when you were single you could easily walk away from an argument...now as a couple you have to think, act and make decisions as a unit, it's not just you anymore you have to make decisions that are in the best interest of you both; you are accountable for each other; you have to deal with conflicts together and no there is no walking away when times are tough; in fact it's the tough times that solid long term marriages are built upon. Be patient, have faith, hope and communicate with one another, remember this is new for you both—and most importantly keep God first, pray together—because marriage is not for the weak it is for the brave and in order to sustain a healthy loving marriage you must stay tapped into the source of unconditional love - God! Stay prayed up and fight for your love and marriage."

– Towandaism

Envision IT!

Manifest IT!

ACTIVATE IT!

What's going to be your "go-to" word today?

"Sending healing love, prayers and comfort, God answers prayers; so, I'm decreeing and declaring you are well and whole in every part of your body! I speak light, love, life and enlightenment over your mind, body, soul and spirit, you have earned your wings, but not today; we need you here, your children need you, your grandchildren need you, your partner in love needs you and your family & friends need you! Please rest up, heal up and then get up because you have so much life to live...be well my friend." – Towandaism

Envision IT!

Manifest IT!

ACTIVATE IT!

What's going to be your "go-to" word today?

"Surely, Lord, you bless the righteous; you surround them with your favor as a shield"- Psalms 5:12 God's – "FAVOR is worth more than money, is more precious than gold and offer you more protection than any man's military and is impenetrable." – Towandaism

Envision IT!

Manifest IT!

ACTIVATE IT!

What's going to be your "go-to" word today?

"The main issue with our world, is that we are trying to fix our spiritual problems with man-made tools!"

– Towandaism

Envision IT!

Manifest IT!

ACTIVATE IT!

What's going to be your "go-to" word today?

"Thank you, God, for the doors you closed to protect me and Thank you for answering **NO** to protect me from things I thought I wanted but was not good for me! To God be the Glory, I am still standing! Amen!!!!" – Towandaism

Envision IT!

Manifest IT!

ACTIVATE IT!

What's going to be your "go-to" word today?

"Stop borrowing from your future to pay for your past and present; don't bankrupt your future and have your blessings arrive empty!" – Towandaism

Envision IT!

Manifest IT!

ACTIVATE IT!

What's going to be your "go-to" word today?

"Gossip is just like junk food, it taste good when you eat it, but it's bad for your health; gossip is bad for your spirit of success, so guard your mind, body, soul and tongue...life and death is at the tip of the tongue—speak life, light, love and enlightenment over your day, home and workplace!"

– Towandaism (Oh, and BLOCK negativity and negative people like a BOSS!)

Envision IT!

Manifest IT!

ACTIVATE IT!

What's going to be your "go-to" word today?

"Please tell me whose life is worth more? We must fight against hatred and bigotry with every fiber of our being and practice Agape!" – Towandaism

Envision IT!

Manifest IT!

ACTIVATE IT!

What's going to be your "go-to" word today?

"Sometimes I just look up and say, 'Now, God, you just Showing Off!' Thank you, Lord! If God has done the same for you say Amen!" – Towandaism

Envision IT!

Manifest IT!

ACTIVATE IT!

What's going to be your "go-to" word today?

"The dark rubs in me! My light is battling ferociously to expose every dark corner, the darkness cannot hide! Divine light fills me up, surrounds me and flows from me to every person, place and thing I encounter...the dark will never win, because I was born from God's light and I remain covered by his Light!" – Towandaism

Envision IT!

Manifest IT!

ACTIVATE IT!

What's going to be your "go-to" word today?

"God can take whatever he wants from you and your life; God could have made us all drones or puppets; BUT, instead, he gave us CHOICE because he doesn't want to control us, he wants to transform us and he wants us to come to him or follow him because we want to, because we desire him so much that we are drawn to him." – Towandaism

Envision IT!

Manifest IT!

ACTIVATE IT!

What's going to be your "go-to" word today?

"Are You wrestling with something, are you suffering, failing; have you hit a brick wall in your career, business; are you in financial troubles, marriage troubles? On behalf of God, I offer the K.I.S.S. Principle--*Keep It Simple Servant!* The answers you seek are in the Bible, Torah, Koran; stand on his word." – Towandaism

Envision IT!

Manifest IT!

ACTIVATE IT!

What's going to be your "go-to" word today?

God said to Moses, "I am who I am. This is what you are to say to the Israelites: I am has sent me to you." (Exodus 3:14 NIV) – "This is why 'I AM' statements are so powerful, purposeful and filled with limitless power and possibilities!" – Towandaism

Envision IT!

Manifest IT!

ACTIVATE IT!

What's going to be your "go-to" word today?

"Hide me God in the GAP (God's Anointed Place) to prepare me for my appointed place." – Towandaism

Envision IT!

Manifest IT!

ACTIVATE IT!

What's going to be your "go-to" word today?

"Lord, help my purpose move from my head, to my heart, to my hands daily! Amen and   Amen!"

— Towandaism

Envision IT!

Manifest IT!

ACTIVATE IT!

What's going to be your "go-to" word today?

"Lord God let it be in your timing, because I would rather stay right here, in my mess, and be in your constant presence than to gain all the wealth and success in the world and not be in your presence."

– Towandaism

Envision IT!

Manifest IT!

ACTIVATE IT!

What's going to be your "go-to" word today?

"You're in a season of becoming; surrender to it with grit, grind and grace." – Towandaism

Envision IT!

Manifest IT!

ACTIVATE IT!

What's going to be your "go-to" word today?

AFTERGLOW

"A life-inspiring book that contains an abundance of positive wisdom. Whether you are looking for a pick-me-up or a life-changing guide, this book will help you succeed. At some point, life's challenges weigh us all down. Many are content to wallow in defeat or accept the status quo of untapped potential as good enough. Not Towanda Livingston. When life beats her down, she finds a way to lift others up. She gets it. By giving to others, she receives. In this book Towanda shares her secrets for turning downtimes around and achieving whatever goals and dreams you have – No matter how small or big, this book will inspire you!" - Nancy LaJoice

"We think, perhaps, a younger person struggling with their destination in life may find help or inspiration from your words, especially your "Towandaisms". They are powerful, uplifting and motivational. The themes you outlined in your book will help guide them in writing their daily journals." – Arlene Venditti and Berniece Smith

"Your "Towandaisms" show one's value from a heavenly to earthly perspective. Page 5: last paragraph gives a life line to someone struggling. You encourage readers to move forward today. Remind them that past experiences are temporary and are building blocks for who they are and their ultimate destination. Success needs basics like knowledge, talent, resources, but these are useless without common sense. Dreams/success are a process – each person arriving in their own way and timing. Stay divinely focused, serve others so that our success will be unstoppable. Change and risk taking are key elements in achieving success. Fall down in failure; get up in victory. The brevity of life should remind us to 'be all we can be.' The spiritual themes and quotes are relevant to our past, present, future and above all our eternity." – Regina Petite

"Towandaism meets you on whatever path you are on, in your life's journey. It is gritty, raw, and real. At the same time, it is refreshing, uplifting, and liberating. The book compels you to go deep inside yourself, into the crevices of your being, and you can't help but emerge with a brand-new perspective of where you are, where you want to be, and your plans on getting to that place. It reminds you that, in the words of the late great Bob Marley, 'None but ourselves can free our minds', and forces you into self-care and wholeness of being." - Sheryl C. Mattis, President/CEO, SherAl Consulting Services, LLC.

"This book is honest and straightforward, and immediately captured this reader's attention. The conversation throughout is frank and tough, no holds barred, and to-the-point. I really liked the concept of identifying and acting on a "go to" word to maintain focus and avoid distractions throughout the day. Each Towandism is impactful and shows readers how to get motivated and find their direction. Especially powerful were the areas on overcoming setbacks and challenges. The book is presented from the aspect of everyone being on a journey, and there being mountains that must be negotiated and overcome along the way. The Towandisms help to successfully maneuver these obstacles. Another concept presented in the book is one of breaking down barriers and freeing oneself of self-limiting thoughts, in order to realize one's full potential. The Towandism action steps provide honest and no-nonsense advice on how to find the path towards a truly meaningful life, and one which brings value to others. The author's sharing of her own experience brings a personal and relatable touch to the story being told. This is a book that will give readers the confidence to overcome challenging obstacles, and appreciate inner strength not previously realized." – Marcia Tucker

"Grit, Grind, & Grace is an awesome motivational self-help tool! Having a 'go-to' word each day has made a huge difference in my work and personal life. I am now able to complete my daily goals by merely focusing on my go-to word and ignoring those less important daily disruptors. Towanda, thank you for my new daily FOCUS lenses!" - Maxene Bardwell, CPA, CIA, CFE, CISA, CRMA

My Dearest Friend and Source of My Inspiration,

I pray you have enjoyed this reading experience, this journey, and this time we have shared together. I don't care how many books you read, there is only one book that has all of the answers, my friend, it is the Bible. From the Bible to the best-selling book today the answer to why you are failing or succeeding is the same, why you are excelling or declining, why you are growing or dying, why you are progressing or regressing, why you are thriving or just surviving…the answer is the same, *as you believe it shall be*. Here's the real, your mind is a trillion times more fertile than the healthiest earth, **whatever you plant**, good or evil, positive or negative, and healthy or toxic it will grow. That **stinking thinking** will derail your journey because no matter how hard you try to succeed, you will fail because you don't believe, don't have faith or hope…you have subconsciously (and some consciously) planted self-defeating and self-sabotaging seeds that have overgrown in your mind choking your dreams and divine planning.

No matter what life throws at you, you were built for this time, reason and season. A confluence of your purpose, passion and possibilities is happening at this very moment; this convergence is pushing you to **ACT!** Every moment you suffered: all the pain; all the loss; all the heartache; all the desperation; and all the stress will pay up today, if you **ACT! YOU**, my friend, are self-made, you are a culmination of your choices thus far; and if you want to change your circumstances make better choices, change your circle of influence, and **INVEST** in you. You have put in the sweat and emotional equity, now, it is time to claim your ROIs (return on investments)! You have earned every blessing, every success, every moment of joy, happiness and love…**CLAIM IT NOW!**

My friend, warrior, champion, **YOU** have just finished yet another self-help, motivational, inspirational book; and yet and still you have not **ACTIVATED** the greatness in you. What is it going to take to push or pull you off of your mental lazy ass? What and **WHO** are you waiting for to come rescue you from yourself? My friend, I love you, Yep, I truly love you, if I didn't love you, I would have never shared my innermost thoughts, failures and successes with you in this book. I am not talking about that warm fuzzy love; I am talking about agape, real love, the kind of love that calls you on your bullshit, the kind of love that keeps a roof over your head, food in your belly and push you kicking in screaming into your endless seasons of prosperity, abundance, wealth, success, excellence, healing, building, positivity, faith, hope and love.

It's time to clean house, it's time to get your mental (and some physical) house in order, and it's time for you to let go of all the people, places and things that do not support your **QUANTUM** Leap into your divine purpose. It's time to serve eviction papers to toxic friends, thoughts, past, environments, and possessions. Stop trolling empty people, places and posts and start strolling into your continuous successes.

Unfortunately, my Friend, no one can do the spadework for you – I can't lose the weight for you, I can't exercise for you, I can't go through the divorce for you, I can't take the test for you, I can't stop your stinking thinking, I can't stop the pain for you, I can't fight your internal battles for you; and, similarly, I can't claim the blessings, wealth, testimony, prosperity, joy, hope, love and successes that has been anointed and assigned to you. Only you can claim VICTORY! My hope and deep burning desire for you is that you leave this earth empty of all your possibilities, talents and greatness; my hope is that you break free from generational, mental, financial, depressing, painful and oppressive bondage; and my hope is that you become a game changer, way-maker, champion, rainmaker, ambassador, servant and messenger of HOPE, LOVE and FAITH!

Pray with purpose, plan with purpose, act with purpose, and receive with purpose.

To God be the Glory! I pray God finds you where you need to be.

Keep Shining and Showing Up Great!

Many blessings,

Towanda R. Livingston
Activation Coach/Friend/Sister

Generational Curses Broken!

ABOUT THE AUTHOR

Towanda R. Livingston is an award-winning Equity, Diversity and Inclusion Executive. She is an innovative thought equity, inclusion and supplier diversity leader of this era. Since beginning her professional career, Towanda has delivered transformational solutions for corporate and government agencies within the inclusion and supplier diversity space.

Towanda has received numerous awards and industry accolades for developing, implementing and institutionalizing various diversity initiatives and programs for her work in communications, human capital management, and supplier/business and community outreach. She possesses over 25 years of experience and has become a sought-out expert on advocacy and policy development, diversity and inclusion, economic development, business development and organizational strategic planning and management.

One of Towanda's colleagues stated, "the breadth and depth of her experience, in particular, with advocacy, strategic planning and implementation of sustainable economic development, business development, diversity, inclusion and equity programs has been extremely valuable to our organization and those stakeholders fortunate enough to procure her services."

Towanda is a highly skilled and accredited international *"Activational"* life and business coach/consultant, motivational and business public speaker, published author, rainmaker and trusted business mentor. Her passion for what she does is grounded in our unshakeable faith in God.

"Either by inspiration or desperation you will be PUSHED into your PURPOSE." – Towanda R. Livingston

Towanda has journeyed through progressive years climbing the proverbial "corporate ladder" that remains a persistent challenge for women of color. Towanda leveraged this challenge when she realized there is more power and influence in constructing your own ladder through her mindset and actions that have served to help women (and men) of color ascend the ranks in corporate, government and entrepreneurship. Towanda has been affectionately called the "pied-piper" of small, minority and women businesses due to her staunch advocacy of efforts to ensure inclusion of these businesses in contracting opportunities with government, private and public organizations. Towanda has been referred to as "one of the luminaries who has blazed the path of righteousness to increase economic inclusion during her professional career which includes both government and corporate" by the Maryland Washington Minority Companies Association (MWMCA), a premier and influential business association based in Maryland.

Towanda has published a 15-episode podcast series, entitled, *"Waging War on Wealth – Leveraging Supplier Diversity Programs"* that is available on Anchor©, Apple©, Spotify© and other platforms. This 12-part podcast series, equips, enables and empowers small and diverse businesses with information and resources to support them in doing business in the government, private and public sectors. Towanda's most recent published work *"How I Slayed Her"* can be found in a book, entitled, *"Fifty & Fabulous"* an anthology authored by Dr. Sharon H. Porter. In this short story Towanda gives readers an intimate glimpse of her story and some pearls of wisdom.

Towanda is the Chief Business Strategist at **Livingston Worx**, LLC., a company she founded in 2017. Livingston Worx delivers innovative and transformational Equity, Diversity and Inclusion solutions to the government, public and private sectors. Also, Livingston Worx delivers strategic, tactical and innovative solutions to small, diverse and women-owned businesses to help start, sustain and grow their businesses in various marketplaces. Livingston Worx supports small, diverse and women- owned businesses with gaining access to contracting opportunities in the government, public and private sectors.

From July 2018 to September 2019, Towanda was the Senior Director of the Office of Economic Opportunity for the City of Philadelphia. She served as the primary Leader in implementing and overseeing inclusion-related programs that are guided by the City of Philadelphia's legislative mandates and requirements. Under Towanda's leadership and stewardship, in Fiscal Year 2019, the City of Philadelphia achieved 35 percent in minority, women and disabled (M/W/DSBE) participation in contracting for the first-time in the history of the City's M/W/DSBE Program.

Prior to working for the City of Philadelphia, Towanda served as the Director of the Washington Suburban Sanitary Commission's (WSSC) Office of Supplier Diversity & Inclusion (OSDI), from November 2006 to November 2017. In 2017, Towanda hit the $1 Billion mark; meaning during her career at WSSC 2006 through 2017 she has been integral to over $1 Billion in contractual payments to Minority/Women Business Enterprise Firms and Small Local Businesses. Prior to WSSC, Towanda served in various progressive roles at PECO Energy/Exelon Corporation. She has won numerous awards and accolades over her career; and has volunteered numerous hours to community-based organizations that are dedicated to women, children and entrepreneurial causes.

www.ingramcontent.com/pod-product-compliance
Lightning Source LLC
Chambersburg PA
CBHW062031090426
42740CB00016B/2884